THE ENTREPRENEUR'S GUIDE TO

BECOMING A

B.O.S.S.

BUSINESS OWNER STRIVING FOR SUCCESS

Written By:
Martina C. Young

Harris,
thank you for your support
and kindness! Lets go all
the way to the TOP!

© 2017 by
Martina C. Young

Printed in the United States of America

THIS BOOK IS NOT INTENDED TO BE A HISTORY TEXT. While every effort has been made to check the accuracy of dates, locations, and historical information, no claims are made as to the accuracy of such information.

Book Category: Business & Economics, Business Development

For book orders, author appearances and interviews, contact author:

We Are B.O.S.S. LLC
Martina C. Young
2295 Parklake Drive, Suite 550
Atlanta, GA 30345
(404) 857-2677
gettrained@martinayoung.com
www.martinayoung.com

ISBN-13: 978-0692045428
ISBN-10: 0692045422

First Edition

DEDICATION

I dedicate my first book to my children, **Lana and TJ**. *You make my life worth living, and are the reason why I grind so hard. You are my heartbeat and the legacy of all that I have done right in my life.*

ACKNOWLEDGEMENTS

Ron Young, this would not have been possible if you did not give me the support to build We Are B.O.S.S. LLC, and provided me the opportunity needed to focus on it fully. I am forever grateful.

To my Dad, the late *Maurice S. Almand, Jr.*, you taught me everything I know about business. I am living your dream and doing what makes me happy, so I know you are happy too.

To my Mom, *Mary Almand*, you have supported me in every single endeavor, 17 businesses to be exact! Your love and care has always been my backbone!

To my bonus parents, *Ronald and Ida Young*, thank you for always encouraging me and loving me as your own.

Aunt Mileta Smith, Auntie Chanel Payne-Stewart, Uncle Marc Almand, Uncle Steve Brewster, and my cousin *Lana Brown*, thank you for all your advice, time, finances, and love!!

To my best friends that held my hand through the birthing of this book, *Nia Danielle, Adriane Baker, Trina Alston*, *Chantile Gaskin, and Alisa Boykin,* you ladies mean the world to me!

To my PUSHERS – *Kimberly Jones, Jonathan Wofford, Candice Maddox,* and *Jasmine Dudley* – you all wouldn't let me quit!

NONE of this would be possible without giving Glory, Honor, and Praise to *God my Father, Jesus Christ my Savior,* and the *Holy Spirit my Comforter*! I am grateful for the gift and call you have placed on my life!

The Entrepreneur's Road Map

FOREWORD

Success is a relative term. Who you are, what you do, and your personal expectations all must be considered when deciding when and if you have reached that predetermined pinnacle of success for your life. Even though we all have different concepts of what it means to be successful; there are some basic steps that are necessary for anyone trying to achieve their life's goals. In my opinion, one of the most important steps include surrounding yourself with the right people who can point you in the right direction as you attempt to figure it all out.

For many people, the problem is not figuring out *WHAT* success is for them, it is *HOW* to achieve it. As a Master Life Coach, I have worked with many people who have lofty dreams of becoming great entrepreneurs, but are clueless about the process of turning their dreams into reality. Becoming a successful entrepreneur requires work beyond *THE WHAT*. This is why I am so excited about Young's book, *The Entrepreneur's Guide to Becoming a B.O.S.S.* It takes you beyond *THE WHAT* into *THE HOW*.

Martina C. Young is an expert in the field of business consulting and coaching. I have first-hand experience in working with her in this capacity, and can attest to her determination of seeing others win in business. *The*

Entrepreneur's Guide to Becoming a B.O.S.S. is evidence of that passion that has produced success stories for business owners who were searching for answers. Young has laid it all out in terms that are easy to comprehend and execute for that individual who need systematic instructions in building a business that will last.

The book that you hold in your hands is a game-changer. It will guide you through the process of entrepreneurship from A to Z. As you strive to achieve new levels of success and become a B.O.S.S., I am confident in saying that if you follow the instructions included in this manual, you will see your life and your business transform right before your very eyes.

Now roll up your sleeves, take a deep breath, and embrace the journey of becoming a B.O.S.S. – *a Business Owner Striving for Success!*

Kimberly Jones, CMLC
Master Life Coach
Living on Purpose Life and Empowerment Coaching, LLC

INTRODUCTION

At the age of 14 years old, I was introduced to what being an entrepreneur was all about. My father had many businesses throughout his life, but it was at that age that he brought me into his world. I had the blessing of having parents that taught me the principles of business, what it takes to be an entrepreneur, and the practicality of building it from scratch. I always knew that I would never work for another person for the rest of my life; working for someone wasn't my destiny. For five years I learned from dad until he passed away when I was only 19 years old. All the values he taught me are what I carry today.

When I began to work my business full-time, I realized that there were so many others who did not have the luxury I had of learning business at such a young age and many who were lost in what they wanted to do. Along my journey I was mentored by other entrepreneurs and business owners; all the while, still realizing that everyone hasn't been given such an opportunity. I have gone through hundreds of situations either directly or indirectly and it has allowed me help others. Clients have said to me over the years that I need to put my experiences in a handbook that entrepreneurs and business owners could have. What you are holding in your hands is the result of 'listening' and not 'fighting'.

As you delve into this book, understand you don't have to read it in any certain order. It is meant to help you at your current need. I have taken true stories, true scenarios, and have put them in this book for you. What you will find is yourself in some of these situations and the We Are B.O.S.S. Evaluation which is our advice or approach to how we would handle it if you were our client or if it were happening to us as a company as well. Please understand that while there are several ways to handle or resolve a situation, I have included what I thought was the most important. The beauty of this journey you are about to go on is discovering the creativity in business to get the best result out of a bad or complex situation.

Every entrepreneur and business owner should have a guide book, a navigation system of some sort. The goal of this book is to be easy to read, easier to understand, and even easier to implement in any business situation you identify with. It's raw, candid, and very honest. Take your time and enjoy!

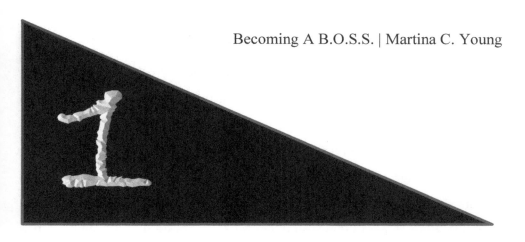

WHICH ENTREPRENEUR ARE YOU?

You woke up one day and decided you wanted to be an entrepreneur. Someone told you how glorious owning a business could be. For several years you have watched countless others work for themselves…some failed, some succeeded, and some just kept going through the motions. You came to this place of reckoning because you always knew that you couldn't work for someone your entire life or you just got fired and have vowed to never work for someone again, or you know that you must do what you can to build this business while working a full-time job. Either way you have decided that you want to step out into the world of entrepreneurship.

CONGRATULATIONS ON YOUR DECISION!!!! Welcome to the world of uncertainty, grind, persuasion, hard work, pessimism, optimism, stress, love, camaraderie, focus, competition, risks, money spent, money earned, design, decisions, partnerships, separations, support, lack of support, creativity, road blocks, desire, planning, dreams, strategy, marketing, accounting, napping instead of sleeping, quick bites over full

15

meals, technology, social media, broadcasting, advertising, long nights, no weekends, flexibility, strict timelines, laws, insurance, reviews, and oh so much more!

You have just joined a very elite group of people in which only a very small percentage of entrepreneurs remain after just one year on this roller coaster. As an entrepreneur, you will bleed and breathe this business every day unless you came to play and then you are no more than a hobbyist. It's important to know exactly who you are, what kind of entrepreneur you are, and if you truly have what it takes to become a serious entrepreneur. Knowing where you fit in will help you understand your strengths and weaknesses. This also will help you to find out how to overcome obstacles that you may face and reduce excuses. Excuses? Yes, excuses!!! Every entrepreneur has their own set of excuses that emerge and knowing how to cut them off at the pass is very important to your success.

The Hardcore Entrepreneur

You are the 'regular people' repellent! When someone asks how you are doing, you tend to answer the question in direct relation to your business. You eat, sleep, dream, talk, and write about your business. Your passion for your business is so powerful that it becomes infectious. You are a walking poster board (advertisement) and anyone who mentions your name can't help but plug your business too! The Hardcore Entrepreneur has tunnel vision, doesn't work a job and puts all cash on hand into the business. The mindset that you have is that failure 'IS NOT AN OPTION'. There is no Plan B, let alone a Plan C! When you think about your life, working for someone else isn't part of it. Every fiber of your being is consumed with your business, making money, getting clients, and doing whatever it takes to make it happen.

The downside of being The Hardcore Entrepreneur is that you tend to isolate yourself from those close to you. If you are married, then you have just taken on a new spouse and this spouse is quite demanding; if you have children then you have just brought an even more challenging child into the fold that requires just as much if not more TLC. Many of your friends don't even know how to relate to you because you can't 'Netflix and Chill' or have 'Dinner and a Movie' or take a classic 'Road Trip', without giving thought to what will become of the business. You also begin to opt out of fun stuff to attend conferences, trade shows, mastermind meetings, and networking events all to grow your business.

You are relentless in your pursuit! Every person you meet is a potential contact or client. People begin to avoid speaking with you, they run the other way because they just want regular conversation and interaction. The Hardcore Entrepreneur operates at another level of dedication to the dream, the vision, and the purpose. You will tend to exchange passion for stress; creativity for road blocks; defining the brand for housing non-related businesses...LOSING FOCUS. The misconception is that being such a Hardcore Entrepreneur leads to true success but unmanaged it can lead to a hard FAIL.

I'm All in but...Entrepreneur

You are the 'excuse on the ready' person! You want what The Hardcore Entrepreneur has but you have gone through so much that fear and unbelief guide you. You believe wholeheartedly in your business but the walls you have put up prevent you from working on your business full-time. You have all the documentation, marketing collateral, a logo, a website, social media outlets, business cards and everything that shows the world you are in business. However, you have limits…show me some money and make me a believer. There is only so far you are going to go because you just aren't going to risk it all anymore. Other things that come up can take priority over your business and you stay in the 'planning phase' for quite some time. You enjoy the idea of having a business and looking the part, yet you are reluctant to be committed to getting too much business. You still want your life to be your life and not be so consumed with the business. Being busy in the business is appealing but having one foot in and one foot out keeps you from truly giving it all you got. You aren't afraid of success, you are just reluctant to truly risk it all. Having your job or other income earning sources is what keeps you secure.

The downside of being The All In but…Entrepreneur is that you tend to second guess the business' potential. You know in your heart that it could be very successful but the failures of the past OR of others keeps you paralyzed from moving forward at full speed. You have no problem spending money to attend conferences, seminars, or networking events because you DO have a true business. However, the money is wasted because you aren't fully vested which results in avoidance of taking on customers. The business has all the makings to be profitable, but you don't know how to kick the BUT out and be all in, fully vested in the business to realize its full potential. The misconception of the 'Being All in but…Entrepreneur' is that you believe by being overly cautious you will guarantee success.

Half-Hearted Entrepreneur

You are the 'let the mood suit you' person! In most cases you are tired of working for someone else and really know you should have a business. Your mindset is always that life must be better than this and no one is going to dictate what your income is going to be. You like dreaming, you've even done a little planning but the follow through to getting the business going full-time always stalls. Situational circumstances dictate your motivation as to whether you want to do what it takes to get the business moving. You have a great idea, product, and/or service…YOU KNOW it will make money! A lot of times you irritate yourself because you can't figure out why you refuse to commit to really getting the business off the ground. After all, you have gotten some business cards through a cheap online service, you built a website on a do-it-yourself type provider, and you talk about your business when the topic comes up.

It drives you crazy that you can't be more focused. Your lack of commitment makes it hard to attain your goals. Your heart's desire is really to have a business but the motivation to do so is flailing. You may be working a full-time job or have a ton of other responsibilities with family and life. The people close to you are always telling you that you need to get the business running. They also remind you that you have a great idea or inquire as to when you are going to get it done. Your heart is split, and you are extrinsically motivated by brief or momentary epiphanies. When

19

you hear a good speech, or read a good book, even have a great inspiring conversation, you put your super hero cape on and are ready to get the business going. Unfortunately, you lose all momentum when those supercharged feelings fade away.

The downside of the Half-Hearted Entrepreneur is the manifestation of your business is never fully realized. You don't have enough belief in yourself, the business, or discipline to build your business. You will never give it your all and will spend more hours dreaming than pushing to make it happen. Your dreams are big but unfulfilled because you rely on others or situations to push you forward. You know in your mind that you have a purpose, a vision, and viable business but you never find that inner motivation to get it going. The people around you begin to doubt you. They associate you with those people who appear to be serious but are always selling a dream.

Being half-hearted keeps you in a state of confusion, never really knowing if you could really make it happen. This confusion also comes from your emotional response to every life altering situation. If there are problems on your job or you change employment, now you want to focus on your business. If someone you know ventures on their own and becomes successful, then you want to focus on the business. At the same time, when situations in your life correct themselves, you stop working the business.

The Creative Hobbyist Entrepreneur

You are the 'I work for free' person! You typically are very good at creating things that people love. Everyone tells you that you should sell your product and if they had seen it in a store they would buy it in a minute. You may be the one who likes to cook or bake cakes for your friends to enjoy. A lot of time is spent coming up with ways to make people smile. You do it because you love to do it. You are great at it because you have a passion for it. Those that are privy to your creations consistently ask for your ideas or samples.

More than likely you work a full-time job which helps to support the supplies needed to make your products. The money that you spend on materials and/or ingredients are now part of your household budget. Every day you think that you might be able to make this into a business and due to the favorable responses to those who have seen your work, you believe that you will be successful at doing it. You are always trying to test your market. If you make jewelry, you wear your designs everywhere to get attention from those around you. If you bake cakes or desserts, you always volunteer to bring the desserts to every pot luck or party. The thought is, by having more exposure to your products, more people will remember you when they want to buy.

The downside to a Creative Hobbyist Entrepreneur is that you almost always find yourself working for free. You tend to allow your passion to override your price point, negotiating it down to working at cost. No matter how much people enjoy your creations, you dummy-down on the cost because you want to make a sale. You may say, "Wow, I sold that bracelet for $15!"; however, it cost you $40 to make. The fact that someone purchased your product is everything to you. You never really treat it like a business but want it to become a business. When you figure out the cost of goods sold, you become fearful of what you would need to sell it for. You talk yourself out of it thinking that people aren't going to pay that amount for it because they know you made it. You wind up working for free.

Another problem with being a Creative Hobbyist Entrepreneur is that you typically sell to those close to you – friends, family, and co-workers. As much as they support you, they don't want to pay you what it's worth. If you bake wedding cakes, then you know if you purchase one at a bakery, it would cost over $1,000. However, they will approach you for the same cake and offer to pay you $300 and you will accept it! This is the problem that you run into quite often. You also get asked, "If I buy the materials, what would you charge me to make it?" They present it to you as if buying the materials is going to lower your labor costs. In your mind, you want to make it a business, but you don't see how you can do it because you find it hard to make a profit.

Two Full-Time Jobs Entrepreneur

You are the 'always doing something' person. While working a normal day job, you have fully vested into your building up your business. You work seven days a week, you don't sleep much, your eating habits are off, and you sometimes feel like you are running in slow motion. The motivation you have stuns everyone around you. You are good at your job and speak about your business to every co-worker or manager. You aren't silent about what your plans are for your business. More than likely, you have a few customers that you service so when you leave your day job you immediately switch over to being the entrepreneur.

When you are operating in your business you have the same drive and tenacity as the Hardcore Entrepreneur. Your philosophy is that your day job pays the bills, but your business is your legacy. Therefore, you aren't going to put more hours in at the job over that of your business. You won't let anyone out work you. You attend every meeting, invest in training and development, the business is fully set-up and operational, and you give it 100% of your time. You are always doing something, it's never a dull moment around you. Your business experiences moderate growth and you are always open to keeping it moving.

The downside to the Two Full-Jobs Entrepreneur is that you overextend yourself. Your due diligence is respected by those who know you and your clients/customers are even understanding when a deadline gets missed. It's what you do to your body and family that takes the largest hit. Working two full-time jobs means that you are lacking rest. There is hardly ever a time where you are just idle of mind and having fun. Your phone rings constantly, if it is not related to your day job then it's your business. Your life is on call at every waking moment. There are times when customers call you at late hours because they understand that you work a full-time job. At the same time, you must work the business around your hours so when you get to work on a proposal, a client's job or product you are exhausted. The intrinsic motivation is what charges you to muster up the energy to get it done.

Time for yourself is very important but you have a hard time finding where you can carve it out for yourself. When it comes to spending time with your family, you feel guilty because you are always on the move with your job or the business. The flexibility to get things done around the house gets pushed to the side because you don't have a moment's rest. It may cause you to miss your children's events, special occasions and vacations. You're constantly in a state of trying to maintain some sort of balance.

The B.O.S.S. Evaluation

The above types are the most prevalent of entrepreneurs you have encountered or found in yourself. Every type of entrepreneur has great things about themselves and then there are areas that they should pay close attention to. Defining which entrepreneur you are will help you understand the impact that you are having on your business. When we are actively living through our cycle, we often miss the brutal truth of what we are doing right or wrong. We overlook the obvious because we don't see ourselves fully. It's been said that you cannot get to the answer if you do not find out the truth. We must find out who we are to have a successful and viable business.

STOP Do not proceed any further until you have done the below interactive exercise.

Take a moment and write down which entrepreneur you feel you are and why.

_____

_____

_____

How has this impacted your business? What changes do you promise yourself to make?

_____

_____

_____

Please don't skip this step. For this book to truly help you, you need to identify who you are. There aren't any right or wrong answers, this is a personal assessment. We are exposing the truth about you! By doing so will only guarantee success for your business.

FYI...Martina C. Young is the HARDCORE ENTREPRENEUR!

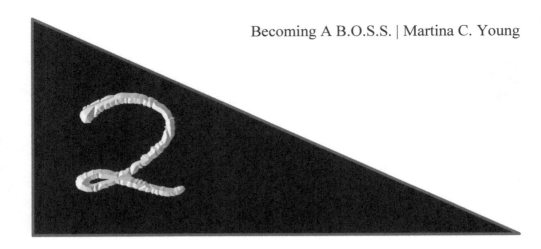

ENTREPRENURSHIP IS NOT "LET'S MAKE A DEAL"

At some point in your life, you are going to have to visit another establishment and conduct an exchange of commerce with a business. This business may be corporately or locally owned, either way there is going to be a transaction consisting of money in exchange for goods and/or services. For example, you have run out of toner and need to go to one of the big-box brand office supply stores to purchase it. You go down the aisle, you select the toner and go to the cashier to check out. The cashier tells you that you need to pay $32.89 and waits for you to run your credit card or hand over the cash. Once you have paid for it, you take your purchase and you leave. Does that sound about right? That's pretty much how it works when we go out into the marketplace and conduct business. There isn't too much negotiation that you're going to do when conducting business in a retail store. The store sets the price and you agree to pay the price. You don't haggle, you don't go to the manager and say let's make a deal. Think about it! You don't proposition these stores to barter services for the product, instead you pay the cost for what you want. That's it and that's all.

Now, what you can do is price compare between the stores, look for running coupons and deals and then make the decision as to which store is going to get your business. My question to you is this, why does it seem that the rules change when dealing with a small business owner or an entrepreneur? Why does it seem that we feel it is OK to haggle another entrepreneur into reducing their price? If we are all in business to make money and YOU want to make money in your business, then why should it be acceptable to attempt to barter services instead of rendering payment? It all comes down to understanding proper etiquette and using this etiquette when dealing other entrepreneurs.

When you are conducting business with another entrepreneur or small business owner it is imperative that you remember how you would want to be treated. I'm not saying that there aren't times when a collaboration of some sort is done, and each party reduces their prices or extends their services – these are not the scenarios that I am referring to. I am speaking of the thoughts that arise and YES, there was point in my life where I had these same thoughts UNTIL it was then done to me!! I can't train you on what not to do and NOT be transparent with you.

When we are starting our business, or we are looking at our bottom line, the first thought we have is how to get it done for less or even for *free*. We begin to think about those we know that can 'use' the business for their portfolio, have a need to prove themselves for referrals, or any other 'pain' we can establish that they might have that will in turn give us what we want. What we don't think about is the time and effort put into the product/service that is being provided to us. What we envision is the 100% profit margin we will be making. Are we thinking of splitting the profit with them? In most times we aren't. However, we begin to think about what we need out of the deal and let the cards fall where they may. Let's take a look at a few scenarios and identify who you are in each one.

Scenario 1 – Michael and Janice

Michael just started a business baking cakes out of his house. He doesn't have a full staff and has to do all the work, the marketing, the deliveries, purchasing the products and everything is his personal risk. He developed a great product that is spreading through his friends and family.

In the meantime, Janice is hosting an event that is costing her more than she budgeted. Each ticket sold included a meal and dessert. Since she can't cancel the event she is looking for ways to cut down the cost and she hasn't even sold all the seats yet. Janice is referred by a mutual friend to talk to Michael about providing the desserts.

The meeting goes well. Michael gives her several options and tries to stay within the budget that she created. Janice gets back to her office and even with the deal Michael is giving her, it's still out of her budget. She comes up with an idea and thinks Michael will have no choice but to go for it because he is still homebased and probably doesn't have expenses like a 'real' bakery. Janice contacts Michael and proposes that he do the cupcakes in exchange for free advertisement on her website, at the event being listed as a sponsor (she will throw in a table too), and allow him the opportunity to post his product on her social media pages.

The B.O.S.S. Evaluation

At first glance this looks like a win-win situation, right? **WRONG!** Michael is risking everything in time, expenses, and liability for the 'chance' that someone will reach out to him based on the event's advertisement or at the *chance* that someone at the event will visit his table and place an order. Janice isn't risking anything at all. It's all reward and benefit for her. She is going to have the event whether the cupcakes are by Michael or store bought. If the event is profitable, she retains the profits and has not made a commitment to compensate him for the cupcakes because she bartered services.

Here's what's missing…if Janice were to pay Michael for making the cupcakes then his advertisement for his business can be branded on the cupcake, the boxes, and if someone asks who supplied the desserts the attendees will still be directed to Michael. At most events, the food and dessert providers are listed anyway. Pay attention to what is NOT being mentioned here and who the true risk taker is in this scenario. *Entrepreneurship is NOT…"Let's Make A Deal".*

Scenario 2 – Michelle and Kate

Michelle and Kate have collaborated on several projects over the years. They have different companies, but they share a lot of the same clients.

29

They both stay in their lane and has made it work for them over the years. Michelle spends a lot of money to attend various conferences, continuing education classes, and is part of many networking groups. Kate on the other hand gets most of her business from referrals and doesn't participate in too many business events because it's just not her thing.

Most of the collaborations come from what deals Michelle brings to the table. Kate suggested that no matter the gig they split the proposal 50/50 and since the business referrals have come from Michelle, she should handle the primary client communications. Kate also gets business referrals from Michelle that may not require her assistance. Kate doesn't give Michelle any type of kick-back AND Kate rarely brings Michelle into a collaboration.

Kate's philosophy is that her assistance is why Michelle closes a client and silently feels that she doesn't owe Michelle a kick-back because without her there would be limited business for Michelle.

The B.O.S.S. Evaluation

If you haven't identified by now, Michelle is taking a beating! Michelle is spending the money to get the contacts, using her time to get the exposure to her target market, and doing most of the leg-work. Kate is simply profiting off Michelle without having to do much work except what she is contracted to do. In no way should she be compensated based on a 50/50 split.

Every idea isn't a good idea and you should never lose control of your business to another entrepreneur. Michelle has allowed Kate to tell her how to run her business. What needs to happen is Michelle needs to treat Kate

30

as a contractor, NOT A PARTNER. She should white-label the services, find out from Kate what her rate is to provide such services and pay her that rate.

It's not Kate's business what Michelle has quoted to the client. At the same time Michelle should be interviewing others who offer the same services to keep her options open. *Entrepreneurship is NOT... "Let's Make A Deal".*

Scenario 3 – Maurice and Lisa

Maurice has an idea to form a community of entrepreneurs that will help each other build their businesses through collaborations and referrals. He hosts meetings that allows every person that comes in the door the opportunity to give their one-minute introduction, pass out their business cards and network among each other. He also provides social media marketing strategies to the group as an added benefit. It doesn't cost anyone to join the group, but Maurice is hoping that through his unselfishness, the team of business owners would refer business to him.

Lisa attends that meeting every week and her business is growing exponentially. She loves how Maurice answers all her questions about building a solid social media marketing campaign. Lisa calls him, texts him and tags him in every one of her posts so that she can leverage off his following. Lisa is hosting a big event that is too large for her to handle so she calls Maurice to get his input. He tells her that he would love to help, but he would need to conduct a consultation for such a project and it would cost her $250. She agrees but Maurice doesn't hear back from Lisa and she stops attending the group meetings.

The B.O.S.S. Evaluation

Maurice caused this problem by muddling the distinct lines in his business services. Hosting a networking group doesn't mean he had to become the free advice King. Lisa was an entrepreneur's nightmare...THE MOOCHER! These are the people who want all the benefits of FREE and never the commitment to PAY. Creating this group was a great idea that Maurice had but he is to blame for allowing himself to be used.

He never should have been provided tons of free information that cost him education, resources, training, development, money, and time to obtain. Lisa had his back as long as he was serving as her personal go-to person, but Maurice had to remember that he was in business to make money. Moving forward Maurice needs to beware of the moocher. He should at least charge a nominal fee for people to join the networking group and modify what information it offers to those who attend the group. This will send a clear message that he is in business to make money just as they are. *Entrepreneurship is NOT... "Let's Make A Deal".*

Scenario 4 – Belinda, John, and Carol

Belinda and John are looking for someone to design custom robes for their church's choir. The pastor has given them a very strict budget and he will not approve anything over the amount discussed. They meet with a fellow church member, Carol, who has her own business as a seamstress and designer. They figure since she is a church member they might be able to get a good deal by going with her.

Carol has a staff of ten people that work for her, she has a professional retail location in addition to the other expenses that go along with a business like hers. Belinda and John explain the situation to Carol and tell her that the pastor isn't moving off the budget. Carol tells them that what they are asking is impossible to have done for such a low budget. She offers them an alternative which will result in a lower quality and it would have to be done by an outside company. John tells Carol since she is a member of the church they should get a discount and not have to settle for a cheaper product. Carol wants to help so she offers a few additional options that will still result in more costs on her end and literally no profit made.

The B.O.S.S. Evaluation

Being a member of the church or any other organization does not mean you are mandated to discount your services. It isn't fair to Carol that because she has a business, she is expected to take a loss because of the organization's budget. In these cases, you should find out the company's cost and if it exceeds your budget then simply say, "It's not in our current budget."

Never make an entrepreneur feel obligated to provide special pricing or to take a loss because of affiliation. If you can't afford a product or service, then maybe you need to review other areas of your budget to cut to find the money. You should never think it's okay to guilt trip an entrepreneur into lowering their price or taking a loss ESPECIALLY if you, yourself have a business.

In this case Carol still wanted to help and gave them a reference that may not give them the quality they expected to get with her, BUT she didn't leave them without any options. She broke the entrepreneur's rule that you may have overlooked...she gave them a competitor!!! She also offered to do the deal at a loss to her business and did not stand her ground in her business. Always stand your ground in your business! *Entrepreneurship is NOT..."Let's Make A Deal"*.

Scenario 5 – Nick and Sam

Nick has started a promotional company where he is going out on foot passing out flyers for clients. He enjoys having the freedom from being in the office and getting a chance to meet people while he is out working. He went to a networking event that taught them about hiring interns or finding mentees that could help him increase his business because he would be able to serve more clients. Nick did the math, set a goal for income and then went in search to find someone to help him cover more ground. He met Sam.

Sam used to have his own promotional company but couldn't keep up with the demand and wound up shutting down. When Nick presented him with the opportunity to 'help', Sam jumped at the chance. Sam agreed to come on board as a 'mentee' with no compensation for 90 days and then they would discuss it further. Nick added that Sam would be responsible for coming up with his own marketing demographic areas and a tracking method. Nick had never had this in place and figured he would get the most out of Sam since he mentioned he used these things in his prior business.

All was going well, and Nick's business began to grow and profit off what Sam brought to the table. Sam had great faith in Nick until the 90-day timeframe came around. Nick liked making all the money without having to pay anything out, so he informed Sam that his time as a mentee was over and that all the resources he brought to the table belonged to his company and wished him well.

The B.O.S.S. Evaluation

This is a situation that I have witnessed more than I would like to have. Nick took a GREAT idea and used it in a negative way in the end. Using interns and those that want to be mentored is okay, *if* you keep your word and not abuse it. Sam had the key to building Nick's business and forfeited his right of ownership for the strategies he developed (his own special sauce) all for no income earned and no opportunity to earn it with Nick.

Sam was taken advantage of by Nick because Sam didn't realize his own worth and potential that he brought to the table due to having an unsuccessful business before. What Sam could have done was had the conversation with Nick that if coming up with the tracking system and marketing demographic territory was needed that he (Sam) would retain all the rights and ownership of it. This means Nick would either pay Sam to use this method in his business OR pay him to develop one specifically for Nick's business, which would have nothing to do with being a mentee. Know your worth!!! *Entrepreneurship is NOT... "Let's Make A Deal".*

35

At some point, we have all been at least one of these people in the various situations. It's okay if you have been the unfavorable person if you have learned from it and change your behaviors. The reason you don't have to subject yourself to being used and abused is because YOU KNOW WHO YOU ARE – YOU KNOW WHAT YOU BRING to the table. You don't have to scam, bribe, lose your integrity, or compromise yourself to get better prices and services from another entrepreneur. Be honest, walk with integrity, and never be afraid to look elsewhere; it's okay and it will all work out in the end.

STOP Do not proceed any further until you have done the below interactive exercise.

Have you ever been approached to make a deal that compromised your rules? How did it make you feel?

_____

_____

_____

What new rules for your business have you put in place or will you put in place to safe guard yourself from situations like these?

_____

_____

_____

Which scenario bothered you the most? Did you see yourself in that situation? Explain.

_____

_____

_____

Please visit: www.facebook.com/weareboss1 and get the conversation going. Tell us about your experience.

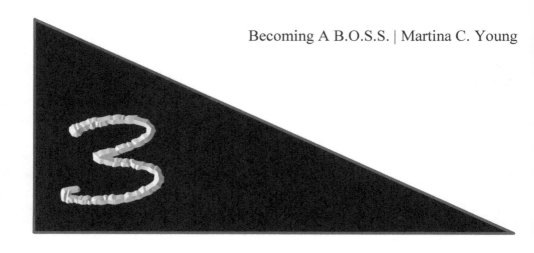

NEVER LEAVE MONEY
ON THE TABLE

Everyone raises their children differently and in my house, we have raised our children to always give those who serve us the tip in their hand. Even if it's on a credit card receipt, they are to place it in the person's hand and NEVER leave it on the table. Money left on the table can be taken by someone else that it was not intended for. The same principle is stated when conducting business...WE NEVER LEAVE MONEY ON THE TABLE! Leaving money on the table means you just shorted yourself and your company the opportunity to make profit or obtain a new prospect.

In many cases you may not even realize where you have left money on the table, you *lost* money; it's a loss! If you were at the bookstore having coffee and you left the five-dollar bill wrapped in the receipt on the table when you left...you would have said, "I left my money on the table" or "I lost five dollars at the coffee house." It's the exact same situation, only we aren't talking about five dollars! Let's look at a few real-life situations where entrepreneurs have left money on the table and what you can do to avoid it in the future!

Scenario 1 – Missed Opportunity

Lana ran a catering business that served comfort food in a very high-end and classy manner. She wasn't a baker, so she shied away from offering desserts. Another customer referred the type of client she really wanted – one with a major budget for a wedding that desired the type of food she made. The meeting was going very good. The bride's mom was very impressed with Lana's options and pricing. Lana knew she was about to book this client and make a killing!

As the meeting was ending the client failed to mention one thing that she needed covered, dessert. The woman's husband said he didn't want to hire multiple companies to provide the food and dessert, he was adamant about using one catering company only. Lana hesitated and advised the client that she didn't make desserts, BUT she could refer the business to a few bakers that she consistently did business with.

The client frowned and said they didn't have time to go through another meeting and her husband really wanted to make this as simple as possible. The client was almost begging Lana to make even a simple cake or cupcakes. Lana apologized but wouldn't relent. She just didn't make desserts. The client said she understood and was very disappointed, but they would need to find another caterer who could meet their needs. Lana was

39

devastated as this gig would have opened greater doors for her and because she couldn't bake, she lost it all.

The B.O.S.S. Evaluation

Lana left the entire check, future business, and referrals sitting on the table. It is understood that she can't bake and if she did, it may not have been consumable to most palates. Lana's lack of creativity and maneuverability to get the job done was the problem. She didn't listen to the client! The client told her that they only wanted to use ONE company for everything. Apparently, that went over her head because her suggestion involved other companies.

What she could have done is found out from the client what type of desserts were desired and then informed her that the desserts were not factored into the initial quote; she would need about two business days to get back with her on incorporating the desserts. This would have given Lana the time to contact the bakeries that she outsources business to, explain the situation and get their quotes. She then could have presented everything to the client by stating that there is a bakery she has hired to handle the desserts but all communication, invoicing, and such would go through her company only.

The client would be getting what they desire by working with only one company, having the main contact person, and Lana could have made a profit off the desserts too…increasing her revenue on the project without having to do the work. It's okay to stick to what you do, but don't lose an entire deal because you aren't being creative enough to make the deal work. Lana didn't have to lose the deal. *Never Leave Money on the Table.*

Scenario 2 – Miscommunication

John and Adam have developed a top-notch platform that provides a business with a program to help with developing a sales funnel. The program will help clients capture the information needed to determine concrete demographics needed to develop a sound marketing campaign through direct mail and social media. Adam is the most outgoing of the two, so he deals more with the customer interaction and direct sales to their potential clients. John is a straight programmer and very introverted. He is passionate about the program he has developed and feels every business owner needs this and if they don't see the value then they obviously have no clue what it takes to garner sales.

Through a conversation with a mutual colleague, Adam meets Victoria. Victoria has two small insurance agencies in the suburbs and is looking for a more effective way to convert leads into customers. Adam's personality wins Victoria over and she believes that they are the company for her to use. She only has one hesitation, because of insurance commission laws she doesn't want to use social media because it would be easier for her to stay in compliance through direct mail or outbound sales. Adam assures her that this program is customizable and won't be a problem for her. She decides to come to the office to get started but Adam isn't there. She meets with John instead. He isn't as friendly as Adam and seems a bit impatient with her questions about the program.

As she is reviewing the proposal she sees that they have incorporated a fee for social media. Victoria informs John that she already had a conversation with Adam that she would not be using this platform due to compliancy issues. John advises her that she doesn't have a choice and the price that she was quoted in her meeting with Adam included the social media program. Victoria is livid because she doesn't want to be charged for something she will not use AND that was not how Adam presented it to her. John informs her that she cannot separate it out and if she didn't want the social media portion then it would be on her not to use it. She rips up her check, calls their business a fraud and walks out the door.

The B.O.S.S. Evaluation

There are so many things wrong with this situation!! First of all, John should never be allowed to talk to a client ever! Sometimes how we deal with a client causes us to leave bags of money in the car because it never even gets to the table. It appears that Adam and John lacked communication which led to Victoria being confused, offended, and upset. Adam should have verified with John whether the program could separate out the services that Victoria wanted to use.

It's okay to tell a client that you need to verify what they are asking can be accomplished. If Adam had done that one step, he could have found out from John and then informed her. If Adam had knowledge that the pricing structure would not change because it was all inclusive, then he messed the deal up by making the client have a different understanding and thereby appearing unethical.

Having been posed with this situation, John may need to go back to drawing board and figure out how to design the program to separate out platforms that clients do not wish to use. This way they could close deals with profit off one platform instead of losing an entire deal and it will demonstrate their versatility.

Scenario 3 – Promoting the Competition

Olivia has just started a t-shirt design company that provides custom shirts for millennials. She makes the designs herself and has the printing press in her basement. While Olivia can't afford to hire anyone at the time, she usually takes smaller quantity jobs that she can fulfill in a five-day window. Her social media page is how she gets most of her business along with being tagged in each of her clients' posts.

Olivia gets contacted by a well-known sorority who has fallen in love with her work. Olivia is excited about the opportunity and the fact that they already have their design and are still willing to pay her fully inclusive price. She meets with the directors of the local chapter and is told that they need to have 5,000 shirts ordered and would need them back within two weeks. They give her all the specifications and Olivia became overwhelmed.

Olivia explains to the ladies that she has never printed more than 100 shirts in any one order and is fearful that she cannot meet their deadline. She further explains that she doesn't have the staff or technology to get the job done. Instead, she tells them to contact another local company that can handle the volume.

The B.O.S.S. Evaluation

Olivia just gave away the business to a competitor. I am not promoting either restaurant, but look at Burger King and McDonald's...do you ever hear a manager at either restaurant tell their customers to go to their competitor? The problem is most entrepreneurs think that by giving the customer a place to go and not leaving them hanging, it will make that client feel that they were being looked out for.

The problem with this is that you have just sent the customer to another place to forge a relationship and you have just told the client all your negatives and allowed them to feel better about NOT CHOOSING you. What Olivia should have done was contact the referring company and established a broker account or find out what type of deal she could broker to get the shirts done.

We leave money on the table when we don't use our creativity to determine how we can make this deal work. It may mean that you don't make 100% of the profit, but if you aren't doing the work then your time is freed up to work on another project while this one is in production by a company that can handle the volume you need with the quality you are known for. Olivia allowed fear to push her away from doing the job and got rid of the client in the process and became an unpaid advertiser for her competitor. *Never Leave Money on the Table.*

Scenario 4 – Not Being Prepared

Alex has just started his business coaching company. He put a lot of time and effort into developing his curriculum. He spent a lot of money on getting all his course material printed, invested a lot of money in social media ad campaigns and began to join many local business groups. Alex was ready for his business clients because he knew he covered all basis.

A director of a very large entrepreneur group contacted him because they thought it would be great to add what he did to their services. They would compensate him for every individual that completed the training. Alex was excited. This meant he wouldn't have to do as much leg work and could have at least 30 new clients each month. He only needed ten new clients to cover all the money that he spent, and he would be in profit fairly quickly.

About two months of negotiations went by and the first group of 15 was ready to begin. He designed the class to be very hands-on, meaning it would be very time consuming for each attendee and that was one thing that Alex didn't anticipate. After two weeks of the first session beginning, six people dropped out of the program. Alex was crushed. The next week eight more dropped out of the class and this concerned the director. He contacted Alex to give him feedback. He told him that the attendees are having a hard time balancing their business, work, home, and school with his program because its demanding at least 20 hours a week of their time.

Alex became defensive because he knew that he had developed a concrete and sound program. He said that his coaching program was built for people who were willing to give their time and energy into growing their business – maybe their attendees didn't understand what it took to become an entrepreneur. At this point the director said they would pay him for the students that attended up to this point but that they needed a more flexible program as previously discussed and they dropped the program.

The B.O.S.S. Evaluation

The sad point in this scenario is that I have personally witnessed MANY business owners suffer from this 'know it all' type behavior. Alex thought he did everything right, but a tremendous amount of money was left on the table for another business coach to come and pick up because he DIDN'T do everything right. Having all your tools in place, looking like a real business doesn't mean you are all there. There isn't anything wrong with the type of coaching program that he developed it was wrong for this client.

Alex could have saved this deal by listening for two months that the client's base needed flexible options. He could have designed a course for these attendees. Alex thought he knew more and therefore wound up not being prepared because he had one product, that was all. Alex could have told the client that his current coaching program required at least 20 hours each week of their time and he would need another month to create something to fit their needs while ensuring they were still getting the same or better results.

This also would have given him ANOTHER COACHING PRODUCT!! In the client's mind, Alex would be creating a product for them; while at the same time Alex would have been able to increase his target market by having a more flexible option! Alex wasn't prepared and was resistant to the feedback he received. *Never Leave Money on the Table.*

Scenario 5 – Lack of Listening

Blake, Todd, and Dalen are looking for a competent contractor to give them a quote on getting some remodeling done in their office. They have just bought a warehouse that is every contractor's dream come true – IT'S EMPTY! The men run a manufacturing company that had out grown their three home garages and basements. Dalen had developed the blueprint to make the business run smoothly and increase productivity by 40%. Dalen was tasked to find the perfect company to build out the warehouse. Blake handled most of the international correspondences and needed to be sure that the offices were soundproof so that business could be conducted efficiently. Todd was more concerned with the security of the building and wanted to be sure that in the build out there were no blind spots whether inside or outside of the building.

The looming problem is that they were in a time crunch and needed to have completed within nine months, which typically a job of this magnitude would take at least a year. They were aware that it was aggressive and were willing to see if they could get it done because Dalen really believed in his blueprint and they needed to increase their productivity.

Dalen met with several companies who pretty much laughed the men out the door with their timeframe and details of the blueprint, until he met Jeff. Jeff had a local construction company and admitted to Dalen that he had never done a job of this size but was confident that he could pull it off. That's all Dalen wanted to hear. He set a meeting up with Todd and Blake to inform them of the good news. He told them that Jeff promised that his team would begin work in the next three weeks and they could make the deadline. What Dalen didn't share with them is Jeff's inexperience.

Having confidence in what Dalen shared, Blake contacted one of his largest international clients and agreed to the terms of their deal. They would be able to fulfill their largest order to date! As work began to unfold, the men were beginning to wonder if in fact they had went with the right company. For this to be such a huge job, the workers were few and deadlines kept being missed. Four months into the project, Todd called an emergency meeting with his partners because he was concerned about the lack of progress. Dalen finally admitted that Jeff told him they had never done a job like this before but was confident that they could get it done and to the specifications of the blueprint. Blake was very upset because this meant they would not be able to fulfill the international order and would have to find another company to get the job done.

The B.O.S.S. Evaluation

You're probably trying to figure out who left the money on the table? In this situation, each of the business partners and Jeff left money on the table. Let's start with Dalen. Dalen developed this beautiful blueprint that would increase their productivity and give the other partners what they wanted in the custom location. The problem is that all the other reputable contractors he talked with before Jeff, found major problems in the blueprint and in the timeline.

Blake and Todd should not have tasked Dalen with being the only one to speak to the contractors or to hire one. That is the beauty of a business partnership, you don't have to make all the decisions and what may be your blindside is your partners' focal point. If they had been a part of the conversation, then they could have talked with Dalen about the blueprint to get it how it needed to be, and they would not have hired Jeff. Jeff entered the picture by knowing his weakness and lack of experience but looking at the money he could earn from such a gig. He took a job that was over his head and would not be able to complete.

The business partners left money on the table by LOSING IT! They lost their time, paid out funds for the work that was in process, and will not meet their largest job. Blake should have NEVER committed the company to the job until they were in true sights of the work being done and passing state/county/local city ordinances. Jeff could have negotiated for a smaller job, made a little money and kept his reputation. You can leave money on the table when you get greedy, when you choose not to seek wise counsel, and/or when you get in over your head. *Never Leave Money on the Table.*

Scenario 6 – Not Following Through

Gladys is an event planner in the Atlanta area. She loves to plan all sorts of events, but her favorites are weddings. Weddings give her more flexibility in client-load management and are more profitable than the other events. The one thing that sets her apart from her competitors is that she custom designs packages for each couple that allows her to give them a unique experience.

During her slow seasons she runs several advertisements for baby showers, birthday and anniversary events. This gives her the needed income to keep afloat until her busy season comes up. Gladys received a request on her website to plan a woman's 50th birthday party. She contacted the potential client and had a meeting. Gladys thought what they wanted was too basic and would be an easy gig. They were planning this six months in advance and the brunt of her work wouldn't be needed until much later. She promised them a proposal by the next business day. Instead she got tied up with other things going on and didn't remember to send the proposal until four days later when they contacted her to find out if she sent it. She apologized and sent it right out. Gladys got the gig but because the money wasn't that significant it wasn't on her top priority list.

Throughout the months Gladys did exactly what she was supposed to do as per her contract, but her timeliness was subpar. Gladys felt that because they had an internet special, she would only do what was required because there wasn't much to get out of this deal. The client couldn't say that the experience was bad, but it wasn't what she had hoped for with Gladys. They were happy to get to the day of the party and it was beautiful, Gladys did a great job for the night and everyone was happy. What wasn't expected is that the client was in on a surprise for her daughter.

When she got up to make her toast to all who came, she instead allowed her daughter's boyfriend to come forward and he proposed. Gladys was so excited because she assumed that they would call her, and this would be the paycheck she wanted. That call never came.

The B.O.S.S. Evaluation

Never under estimate the worth of a project! If you choose to take a less than profitable project or one that you aren't passionate about then you should not change the dedication and commitment to it. Every client interaction should be stellar and one that they can write a GREAT review about. Does this mean that every client is going to be a 100% positive experience? Absolutely not! However, if you do your absolute best then you can hold your head up high knowing that you gave it your all.

If Gladys had treated this client like she did her wedding clients or her more profitable events, then they more than likely would have contacted her to be the event planner for the wedding. She missed promised dates, her energy and communication were subpar, and the client had a mediocre experience. Gladys left money on the table by leading the client away from doing business with her in the future. That would also include not getting possible referrals.

Gladys treated the client as if she were doing the client a favor. It was her choice to offer a deal, it wasn't the client's. If her involvement is based on pricing for gigs, then she definitely needs to stop running specials or taking on events that she is not inspired by. She may have made her income for that birthday party, but she left unrealized earnings on the table by not being her best in business. *Never Leave Money on the Table.*

Understanding that bad business decisions and poor business etiquette can cause us to leave money on the table will only serve to help avoid making those mistakes. It is important for the continued growth of the business that you look at every situation carefully. Never take for granted that your reputation will be the reason that people use your services or that you can force a client into taking the suggestion you have made. Learn to be creative as much as you can to make the deal work. Sometimes that means bringing in others to help you and PAY THEM for it. It's okay to be the expert in your field, but always know that you can learn something, and your way isn't always the best one. Be coachable! *Never Leave Money on the Table.*

STOP Do not proceed any further until you have done the below interactive exercise.

Write at least three instances where you have left money on the table.

_____

_____

_____

Where did you go wrong in those three situations? What is your plan to avoid that from happening again?

_____

_____

_____

_____

_____

Don't skip these exercises!! This is going to help you to ramp up your creativity and contingency plans to avoid losing money.

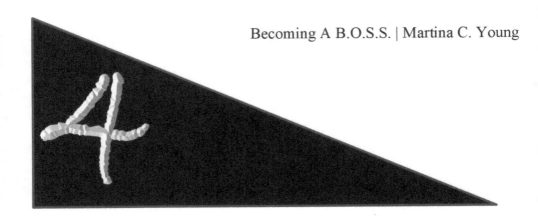

ARE YOU PLAYING OR CONDUCTING BUSINESS?

When we were young we used to play a game called, "Monopoly". That was the game that taught us economics, business, decision making, and consequences. Each person has their own strategy when playing the game because it works for them. Some of us buy up every property on every single turn taken, others of us wait it out to get all the railroads or purchase a specific block of properties; either way we are playing a game to win. The seriousness of each player is what helps make the game all too interesting and in some cases, can cause a very heated exchange amongst players. The point of this memory is that every person comes in to WIN and not lose, we don't treat it like a regular game…we come to conduct business. The same approach should be for us in actual business. We should show up to a place ready to do business and not play a game. The sad fact is many entrepreneurs show up thinking that they are coming to conduct business when in fact that are still playing 'play-play'.

Over the years, I have come across so many people that claim they are conducting business but act as if they are jumping in a bounce house. I love to have fun in business! We all should but if the only thing a person can remember is how great of a story you can tell and neglect to remember what it is you do – then you are playing too much! Below are a few true stories of situations that I have witnessed over the years. For sake of privacy, some of the names and companies have been changed – but the situations are factual!

True Story 1

About two years ago, Daymond John had an introduction event to an academy that he was launching. Now, the advertisement NEVER stated that he would be in attendance, it simply stated that this academy was his and there was a free event that we could attend to learn more about it. I signed up and went by myself, which I hate to do! When I got there, I noticed that there were about two hundred people in attendance, some were dressed ready for success and others were there with their 'clean the house' clothes. You could tell who was expecting to see Daymond and who knew why we were there.

I began to circle the room, it's something that I do often and listen to conversations because I am ALWAYS looking for my target market. I came up on a conversation with a professional looking woman and an even nicer dressed man. The woman is who I am going to focus on. At first glance she seemed like she's been in business for years, she had the look. You know the one with the distinguished suit, a leather brief case, her hair and make-up…flawless. She also had that banker voice, the kind that is inviting and very knowledgeable. The gentleman starts the conversation off by asking what kind of business she has, and this is where everything goes downhill. Let's call the woman Gina and the gentleman, Chad.

Gina begins to tell Chad about her business and how much its growing. She says that she is generating over $12,000 a month in new sales along with growing her current client load. Of course, Chad seems very impressed and begins to talk with her about his business. At that point, Chad takes out a business card, he's holding it in his hands when he asks Gina for hers. He says that he would like to have a meeting with her, so they could talk more about how they might be able to help each other.

Gina pauses for a moment and says, "I would love that but let me tell you what happened. I had new business cards done and the graphic designer didn't get them to the printer in enough time, so I don't have any cards on me. Tell you what I am going to do, I am going to write my information on this (tears off a piece of notebook paper) and you can contact me this week." She doesn't even realize that Chad has put his business card back in his suit pocket.

Gina came to play and not conduct business. Here's the deal, things happen with the printer, we have all been there a time or two. However, Gina knew that information the day before the event and should have taken herself to one of the office supply stores because they even print temporary business cards! There was no excuse for not being ready to conduct business. The next thing is that she said her email address as she was writing it down and it was either a Gmail or Yahoo account. There is no way that a business owner who is operating a $12,000 a month in new sales cannot afford to purchase a $15 domain and get a free email account. If your business is BlahBlah, then she should have had an info@blahblah.com email address. *Are You Playing or Conducting Business?*

When you come to play you aren't ready to conduct business. Chad obviously was thinking the same way because he took her piece of paper and the conversation ended quickly after that. Gina thought by building up her business and engaging him on the money she said she was making, that would give her legitimacy. It worked at first but then how she appeared to be conducting business changed his mind.

If you are a business owner without a domain in your name or in your business name with at least a landing page, then you are playing! Too many times are people relying on having a social media presence but not a website. Unbeknownst to many, there are still millions of people who do not have social media accounts and never will. Gina left money on the table, misrepresented herself and lost out. She appeared to be playing and not conducting business.

True Story 2

It was October 2016 and my cell phone provider announced that they were recalling my newly purchased phone because they were catching on fire. I had a flight to Las Vegas to catch that next week and they said I couldn't carry it on the plane. I had a speaking event for our forming non-profit organization, Junior B.O.S.S., a few days before and had cleaned out my car. When I finished, I decided that I had better get to the store to switch out the phone. When I arrived, I was met by a very nice gentleman that we will call, Trent.

Trent was so helpful and noticed that we had a lot of devices on our plan. I told him that I conducted a lot of business on my phone and he asked what I did for a living. I told him all about We Are B.O.S.S. LLC, and that I am a business coach. He then tells me all about his business idea and that he needs to meet with me. He asks me if I have a business card. Surely, I do because I travel with 25-30 of them in my car EVERYDAY. While he is activating my phone, I excuse myself to the car to get him my business card.

The next thing that happens is the slow montage of the previous two hours when I cleaned out the car. The business cards were in the box and I took the box in the house. Being the crazy woman that I am, I start going through every compartment looking for even one of my old cards...something!!! I can't find anything but a few of my company business pens.

Disgusted with myself, I put on my winning smile and walked back into the store. I get to Trent's station and I tell him this, "Of all things, I just took my business cards out of my car. I want to give you something that will direct you straight to me. Here is my business pen and on it is my website." I hand him my pen and he tells me that he needs to put it in his pocket, so he doesn't use it for a client. I then go a step further. I told him this, "I am a solid business coach who just broke her own rule. May I show you how serious I am about earning your business and showing you that I am who I say I am?" He nods. "Okay, since your phone is right here could you please go search for my website, martinayoung.com?"

He kept saying that he trusted me, and I kept telling him that I needed him to go there. He goes to my site and sees it. I then have him interact on my social media icons from my site. I had him do that because if Trent lost my pen and he forgets my name, then when he goes to use his phone to search for something it will show him the last three searches and because he was using Google.com, he never closed the open tab in Chrome. Since my domain is set to my name, he would have my website too.

Even though I came to the store to get my phone changed, I still made sure to be positioned to conduct business and not come in there playing around. It was my fault for not having my business cards, so it was up to me to make sure that I would still be taken seriously. I was not there to misrepresent myself and made the most of what I could, given the circumstances. I remain ready to conduct business! Since that situation, I make doubly sure that I do not remove those business cards out of the car EVER. *Are You Playing or Conducting Business?*

True Story 3

A lot of my clients are at a stage where they are working a full-time job and working on their business. This means that I must have the flexibility needed to conduct a meeting a few times a month after hours. One evening I had a meeting with James. James worked as a business sales executive for a large cable company in the area and was balancing that job and the business. This night we met at the office in the conference room which has a glass wall, so you can see the lobby and those coming in and out of the other suites. A new tenant had moved into the corner office and we were meeting at about 8pm on a Tuesday night.

The new tenant was a law firm and they hadn't even moved in their furniture. We'll call the new tenant, Tracy. Tracy had come in the office and went in her suite. James asked me if I knew her and I told him that she must be the new tenant, but I hadn't seen her before. About 45 minutes goes by and he sees her walking back out the door. He jumps up, grabs a business card out of his bag and follows her. They talk for about three minutes and he came back smiling. James got the business.

He was not at my office to conduct his day job's business, but he saw an opportunity and he went for it. When you come into a place always be ready to conduct business. James was not there to play. He then gave me a handful of his cards and asked if anyone needed his services would I give them his cards. Tracy wasn't dressed like an attorney that night either. She was dressed like I was when I went to the mobile phone store. Obviously, she wasn't there to play either because she talked to him, set up an appointment and got the deal done.

This is what it takes in business, we must be ready in season and out of season. We should always be ready even when we are on our own time. James worked double time that night. He landed an account unexpectedly in his day job and make great progress for his earning potential in his other business. *Are You Playing or Conducting Business?*

True Story 4

A few years ago, I joined a local chamber of commerce. At first glance the members seemed like a good group of people who were active in their community, wanted to do business together, and were serious about helping each other grow. For the most part this was the case. I had gotten very involved in one of their networking groups that proved to be beneficial at that time. One of the rules of the group was that visitors could attend without joining for up to two visits.

There were, what I call 'business moochers' who would go to every free visit in each chapter and take every opportunity to attend as a substitute for a member who would be absent at a meeting. These people never intended to join the group or the chamber, they just wanted anything that was free. It was how they began to build their business. They came to conduct business for themselves by playing the game on the backs of other business owners' dime. Yeah, we all hear about using other people's money, but this was different. These people would take your business card but NEVER refer out any business and would sales pitch you to death in an area they refused to invest in.

All they cared about were themselves, what they could get and how they could get it done under the radar. That is not someone who is conducting business. Free seems great but what it did in that situation is cause everyone that met them to run and talk about them behind their back. A true business person conducts themselves on the up and up. It's not about how much they can take, take, take, and TAKE! It's also about giving and operating at a level of integrity.

61

When you come to conduct business, you know that there are going to be costs involved and you should be prepared for those costs. Never allow yourself to be taken as a joke because you have developed a reputation as a business moocher. *Are You Playing or Conducting Business?*

True Story 5 – MY STORY

A very dear colleague and friend called me in 2009 and said that I needed to learn how to build websites. He told me that it would help me to get the clients that I wanted and sustain a very consistent income. Hearing this and seeing how easy it could be for me to learn, I dove right in. I was building websites in Joomla at that time. My colleague, I'll call him Darryl, told me that I needed to find templates to use that would ease the setup.

As I began looking for them, they all cost money. I called Darryl and he gave me this website that allowed you to download 'free' templates. I didn't know any better, so I began downloading several of them to be ready for any client that came my way. I thought I was setting myself up to conduct business!! WRONG! I completed a few of the sites and the clients were so happy with them and then something really strange happened; something I wasn't prepared for...the websites started getting hacked!!!

By taking the 'free' or the 'backdoor hookup', the templates didn't receive updates, the Joomla tags couldn't be hidden, and I didn't have a purchased license number to protect it...nothing. By trying to be cheap, I caused my clients to suffer and demonstrated my immaturity with lack of understanding. I was out in these streets playing! I wasn't conducting business! I was giving an illusion of it.

I had to make it right and it cost me a very pretty penny to do so. I couldn't have a reputation that made people question their decision to work with me or that I was building bootleg websites. I had to get my head in the game and make it right. It meant that I had to pay a yearly subscription to a Joomla template designer with unlimited web sites, then I had to reload the licensed version to each client and had to recreate a website for one of them using a newer template.

If I never made those changes by coming out of 'playing' to 'conducting' then I wouldn't have been able to write this book. My business would have failed back in 2009. Always be ready to get it right and fix the brokenness in your business. Take a mirror to your business to determine if you are playing or conducting business. *Are You Playing or Conducting Business?*

True Story 6

Starting up a business from scratch is never an excuse to be playing. I have encountered many new entrepreneurs who have taken the time to conduct their research, they pay for consulting or attend educational workshops, and take their time to fully develop their vision. When you are at the start-up phase of your business you should be very diligent in doing all that you can to get in a position to conduct business.

Kelly joined a network marketing company that sold health products and she was very excited about the earning potential. Many of her associates had joined as well and were already getting people signed up under them and purchasing the products. Kelly wanted to take a slightly slower and different approach to sustain the type of success she envisioned for herself.

The team that brought her in began to think that she wasn't as serious as everyone else and began to give her a very hard time. All the while, Kelly was purchasing the product for herself and monitoring its results. After the course of nine months, she had lost over 40 pounds, was taken off Type 2 diabetes medication and her hormone levels began to balance out. Kelly also attended every 'hoo-rah' meeting and training, she researched every new product and took classes on direct sales. After about 10 months, she began to work the business on her own.

Her team lead could not believe how her network was growing so quickly. Kelly's product sales were the highest of all her team members and even outshined the person that brought her in. After two years, she was earning over $350,000 a year in the company and her team grew by the thousands. Kelly took all the negative comments said about her with stride, she knew that she was ready to conduct business and that it didn't matter what anyone had to say.

Now, the same people that didn't believe in her were begging her for advice. Kelly knew that she needed a solid testimony to boost the product and it would give her the knowledge to explain to customers on how it worked. She also knew that understanding direct sales and the company's business model would increase her probability in closing each deal. Kelly appeared to be playing because others didn't realize what she was doing but she was in it to win it and did so by conducting business with an elevated level of success. *Are You Playing or Conducting Business?*

STOP Do not proceed any further until you have done the below interactive exercise.

In what areas of your business are playing?

_____

_____

_____

What changes are you going implement to overcome those areas?

_____

_____

_____

List your personal views on how you are conducting business in the marketplace?

_____

_____

_____

How do you plan on being taken seriously when you are caught off guard?

_____

_____

_____

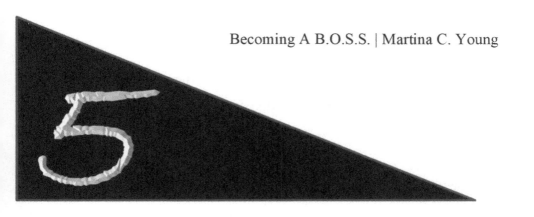

YOU CANNOT MAKE A DEAD HORSE WALK

One of the largest problems in an entrepreneur's business can be their very own team. When starting a business, often we feel that we must include family, friends, spouses, and familiar colleagues to get the business of the ground. We believe in what we want to do (for the most part) but aren't sure we can go at it alone. This causes a lot of us, including me, to make haphazard decisions in bringing people on board. I have done this! I have brought people into my businesses as partners or officers because I lacked the confidence in myself. I can tell you that in almost every situation, the partnership faded.

It wasn't that the others weren't talented or gifted, it was that they weren't supposed to be part of my vision – they had their own path. In a lot of these situations it was like pulling teeth or trying to pick up a dead horse! I am going to venture to say that it is impossible for a human being to physically pick up a dead horse with their bare hands. It's no different than trying to make a bad partnership work. Bad partnerships that I am focusing on are the situations where there is division within the leadership or divided vision. I have witnessed too many businesses become stagnant because of time spent trying to make a dead horse walk. It just doesn't happen, and your business will suffer because of it.

The scenarios you are going to read are going to show you factual situations that have occurred. If you find yourself in any of these situations, then it would be best for you to take some notes on handling it.

Scenario 1 – Indebted to You

Coach Jay was a well-known basketball coach that held tournaments throughout the country. He developed many players that would go on to have successful careers in High School and College. The problem with Coach Jay is that everyone saw his talents but due to his lack of business knowledge he always felt the need to bring others in with him. These were people that helped him to run his programs, leagues, and/or tournaments. The challenge he faced with them is that they didn't have any real skin in the game. They were great at what they offered but they weren't putting up any money, securing any new teams, or even getting gym locations.

Coach Jay began to see a lot of inconsistencies in some of their performances. Some of these people would show up late to the games, failed to follow through with what was promised, and at times would leave the games early. He thought it was possibly because they didn't have ownership of the business and wanted to see about making them a partner. Eve was one of the coaches that he relied on and he presented her with the deal against the advice of his business coach (wonder who she is). He had an agreement drawn up and thought this would solve everything. He would have a business partner that would help him and that she would be even more involved now that she had ownership. Eve agreed to come on board as a business partner, signed the contract and said she was committed to growing the program.

Coach Jay found himself being even more frustrated with Eve because her behavior did not change. In fact, she just wanted to collect a check and if one wasn't ready for her then she had no interest. Coach Jay tried everything to get her to be active and responsible because now people and parents in their program were complaining. Eve was even accused of coming to the various gyms to pick up the door money without allowing it to be counted.

Coach Jay had a big situation on his hands as he really wanted to think that Eve really believed in his program, but she just wanted the financial gain from having a business but contributing nothing.

The B.O.S.S. Evaluation

Eve already demonstrated that she would not be a good fit for the business because she was not a person of her word. Coach Jay was trying to make a dead horse walk in Eve by baiting her with the contract to make her a partner. Eve always showed what she was and what she was interested in, it was Coach Jay who was blinded because of the need he had and what he disillusioned himself to believe about Eve.

The problem this caused was greater than Coach Jay could have ever imagined. He had a brand to protect and by bringing in someone as a partner, her behavior was a direct reflection of the business. Coach Jay would now have to think the best way to have Eve step down from the business.

When you bring someone on as a partner, you cannot just fire them. It doesn't work that easily. What Coach Jay could have done, if compensation is what she needed, he could have hired her AND paid her for the jobs she was doing for him. Personally, I wouldn't have hired her and would have thanked for all the prior help, but we would take it from here. That is what 'Martina' would do and if you were a client of mine, that is exactly how I would have advised you. No matter what you do if a person shows you their inconsistencies early on, make a note...believe it...and move on. *"You Cannot Make a Dead Horse Walk!"*

Scenario 2 – Friendship!

Renee and Kayla had been friends for over 20 years. Both had dreams of creating a baby clothes line that was handmade and made each outfit one of a kind. For years they discussed exactly how they would market the product, who would be responsible for which style of clothes and had agreed that it would be an equal investment for both. Renee fell upon hard times which resulted in her losing her full-time job. She wound up being out of work for a few months and became more motivated to get the product running so she might not have to return to working full-time. Kayla had received a promotion on her job that now required her to travel more and began to put the business on the back burner.

At first Kayla thought that Renee would need to take the time to find another job, so she didn't call her as much. Renee on the other hand kept reaching out to Kayla about the business and was growing aggravated at her lack of urgency with this new position. The truth is that Kayla had lost hope of the business ever becoming a reality and she was dedicating more to her career path at the company.

Renee kept texting her ideas, sending her emails that went unreturned, and even called her multiple times to talk to her about some ideas she had. Renee began to go out on her own to speak with baby boutiques that would be interested in carrying the clothes line, she took her 401K money to attend shows and produced an abundance of products to have on hand. Renee would send selfies and updates to Kayla hoping that it would spark an interest in her again. However, the texts went unreturned and finally she received a call from Kayla asking her only to contact her as a friend, she didn't want anything to do with the business or the product any longer.

The B.O.S.S. Evaluation

In almost all situations, dreams and visions that we have had for decades that do not manifest become to be fantasies. As time moves on, it becomes easier to settle for your life and make forward movements in that only. Kayla more than likely had already started to lose the faith that it was ever going to happen, but it may have been the escape from reality she needed from time to time when talking to Renee.

Kayla may have begun to look at it as more of a hobby. When the opportunity presented itself for her to move up in her job, she could no longer keep up the charade. Knowing that Renee would need to find a job, this was her way out without hurting her friend's feelings. Renee was not paying attention. This couldn't have taken her aback if she truly knew her friend. The passion Kayla had for this business was gone but Renee was trying to get her to come back to the light. What Renee didn't recognize is that there was more action being done and strides being made without Kayla; Kayla had become the dead horse.

There are times when we see that our business partner isn't committed anymore but WE want them to be so bad that we do all we can to overlook their lack of interest. When you have a friend in business, never be afraid to have the uncomfortable conversation. If you are over it, then communicate that you are over it and you might be able to salvage the friendship. When Kayla's resistance became apparent, Renee could have used that time to tell her that she would move on without her and explain her reasons why. More than likely that is all Kayla was waiting on. The burden to make the move isn't going to be on Kayla because she was the dead horse. *"You Cannot Make a Dead Horse Walk!"*

Scenario 3 – MY Story

A few years ago, I felt that We Are B.O.S.S., needed to add another service that would take us into an entirely different and profitable category. Through conversation and observation, I thought about someone who offered this type of service. He was an expert in this industry and without

72

a doubt would be exactly the right fit. He had the outgoing personality that could get us into any room, meet the right people, and secure us the business we needed for this new service. We were very busy. Every week we had meetings to attend, research to conduct, and conversations to be had to get everything moving. The hard part came where there were tasks that needed to be completed, research that needed to be done, and follow-ups that needed to occur. I would send an email asking for an update, we had an organizational manager program that I had available, and would make phone calls. There would always be something else that got in the way of getting this done.

Something else was always more pressing then what needed to take place. I would then have a heart to heart conversation and KNOWING BETTER, I went with his emotional responses and apologies. I went against my own mind and added it to the website, posted it on all social media platforms, and included it into my elevator pitch at networking events. I felt that he didn't understand his full potential and I could help him do it. Needless to say, it was a waste of time and energy, I was pulling a dead horse.

The B.O.S.S. Evaluation

I was doing everything in my power to make this dead horse walk. There are times when we want to expand our business' services and think we have found the person to help us with that. This person was brilliant in his field. The problem is that he tried to have the mindset of an entrepreneur, but he was great at contracting himself out in this field. What I should have done was paid him to consult me on this area of business to see if it really was a good fit and if we could pull it off with the resources we had. I could have also spoken with him to see if we could contract him to perform some of the duties needed.

We (We Are B.O.S.S.), should have worked on making it a profitable business model instead of bringing him in as a partner. By forcing him to be something that he was not 'at the time', only caused him to be more removed and unavailable. It pushed him into a vision he wasn't ready for or prepared to operate in. In this situation, I can honestly say that through seeing 'potential' I assisted in creating this dead weight situation. We are still friends to this day but the burden of building a new business and the responsibilities that aligned itself with that were not his full passion. That made him the dead horse I was trying to pick up. *"You Cannot Make a Dead Horse Walk!"*

Scenario 4 – The Married Couple

Chip and Kara had been married for a little over ten years. When they got married they dreamed of owning a travel agency. Kara had a very good corporate job that provided stable income, health benefits, and would allow Chip to work solely on the travel agency full-time. As they would find out, building a business that is profitable and sustainable for an entire family doesn't happen overnight. There were a lot of tasks that Chip needed to complete to be a certified travel agent, he had to attend many seminars put on by companies he wanted to represent, took classes on how to plan group travel and cruises, and tried his hand at putting many different functions

74

together. They made some money, but nothing truly recouped all that was already invested into the business.

After four years of this, Kara became very impatient with the progress Chip was making. Chip did his very best to keep her in the loop, but Kara was uninterested. He tried to get her to attend certain functions or brainstorm with him, but she just wasn't interested. She wouldn't even hit the 'share' button on a social media post to help push the business. She began to belittle his effort by reminding him that his income did not match hers and it was *his* vision she was supporting. She even went as far as to find it humorous when he would get excited about the potential income he was about to make; she no longer believed in him nor his dreams.

Chip did all he could to remind her that this was a dream they talked about at the beginning of their marriage but all she could say is that it was never her dream, she just wanted to support him. However, when they were in a public group together, she would take all the accolades that Chip was being given by others who used his agency.

The B.O.S.S. Evaluation

This is one of the hardest situations to face when a husband and wife are in business together. It makes it even more difficult when one of the spouses is still in Corporate America and not working in the business daily. In this situation there was an agreement that both parties agreed to and its one that is common among spouses who are in business. The problem arises when one of the partners becomes self-removed.

In this case, Kara was the working spouse. From her perspective, she is the one getting up every day going to work while her patience is wearing thin with Chip getting this travel agency up and running. This is difficult because Chip wants to get his wife involved with the business and it seems as if she isn't interested. For Kara though, it may be like working two jobs now…her 9-to-5 and the Travel Agency.

When you have this situation, it's important to remember that you all are in this together. If one of the spouses is working a day job, then their role should be looked at as the Investor. Give a weekly report to the Investor as to each week's progress or have a physical report for them to review. This helps the Entrepreneur in the relationship to communicate with the Investor and allow them to understand what is going on with the business.

A mistake that I made was not always communicating things with my husband and there were times it caused tension. If we were Chip and Kara, that would have been the way to handle it. When you are business partners, and you are married, if you don't define the roles you won't have the guided peace needed. Stress in a marriage can halt the creativity that is required for an entrepreneur to keep their head in the game. It also doesn't mean because you are married that you must be business partners. It's perfectly fine NOT to be in business with your spouse, especially if they aren't passionate about the business.

Not being in a business partnership doesn't mean that you treat the situation differently in terms of communication, but you lift the 'business partner' responsibility you have on your spouse. Kara didn't have to be a dead horse if this was recognized early on – she became one. *"You Cannot Make a Dead Horse Walk!"*

Scenario 5 – Right Passion, Wrong Business

Max, Andy, and Janine all belonged to a local Chamber of Commerce. Max had a marketing company that he had just started, and he liked to focus on local businesses. Andy had been in business for years as a plumber and was looking to expand his business. Janine was an administrator and organizational management specialist. At every meeting they found themselves either sitting together or hanging out. This would lead to several mastermind sessions about each other's businesses.

Andy was having a hard time keeping his doors open and really needed to increase his clientele. Janine had the idea that to solve his problem, he should take Max and her on as business partners. Max could revamp the marketing and she would get all the administrative and organizational needs completed. It sounded like a perfect match! After a few conversations, the partnership agreement was drawn up and they began working together. In the beginning, it was working out perfectly. Janine made sure that the books were in order, the staff paperwork was done, client contracts had been updated and moved them to an electronic based system. Max rebranded the company, launched a very productive marketing campaign, and gave them an online presence that allowed the company to compete in a new market.

Andy was loving every minute of it as the business was pouring in and they had never been this busy. They were riding this high for almost two years with money being generated and were even considering opening a second location when it all began with a missed meeting here, a missed meeting there for Max. Some days he came into the office and others he opted to work at home. Janine noticed it first because Andy was usually in the field with his team. They would take turns attending different networking events and meetings. Max began missing them and coming up with reasons why he needed one of the partners to cover his absence. Andy was out in the field one afternoon and he saw Max in a business meeting at a coffee shop. It looked like he was conducting a presentation on his tablet and he saw a smile on his face he hadn't seen in a long time.

It turned out that Max had rebooted his marketing business and lost interest in the plumbing company. Andy and Janine thought he might be bored, so they had a meeting with Max to discuss the plans for the new location and they wanted him to come up with everything. Max seemed delighted, but he struggled to come up with a new campaign for it. He struggled to even be there. Janine and Andy were shocked and after a few more meetings decided to let Max out of the partnership.

The B.O.S.S. Evaluation

Max became a dead horse because his passion for marketing was tied to doing so with a variety of local businesses, not beholding to one market. He became bored and unfulfilled in the partnership. Janine and Andy were living their passion every day and seeing the results of their labor. For Max though, his creativity for branding, creating, and planning was being stifled. He tried to commit to the partnership, but it wasn't his full vision. It was a great project at the beginning because he was just starting his business, but he never considered his passion. It was the thing that drove him every day. His passion wasn't tied to marketing for the same company. Money doesn't motivate every move and it doesn't bring happiness as most may think. This is a very common situation that many people have found themselves stuck in.

Andy and Janine may have been afraid to see the full truth because they know a large part of the success was due to the change in marketing. Without Max, would the business still have the same measure of success? This happens when other partners do what they can to keep a dead horse on out of their own fears and selfishness. Creating an opportunity for the dead weight doesn't mean that it will reignite the fire inside of them. It only makes matters much worse than they are. *"You Cannot Make a Dead Horse Walk!"*

Having business partners to help carry the load is very helpful. You just have to make sure that when you make this decision to establish a partnership that you do it after giving it much thought and conversation. Never be afraid to ask the hard questions. Find out what each person's ultimate dream as an entrepreneur is and open the dialogue from there. Avoid bringing on partners when you are desperate for change, have lack the confidence in your own abilities, or see potential in others who do not see it for themselves. If you find yourself trying to resurrect a dead horse or you find yourself becoming the dead horse...STOP and OPEN the dialogue.

STOP Do not proceed any further until you have done the below interactive exercise.

Write out your thoughts on business partners. Do you have any? Are you against having them? How would you recognize a dead horse?

_____

_____

_____

_____

_____

_____

_____

_____

I have a business partner is the dead horse I am trying to make walk, here is my plan to handle this:

_____

_____

_____

_____

_____

_____

_____

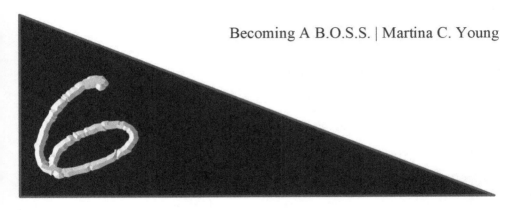

NEVER ALLOW YOUR DREAMS TO BE CORRUPTED

When you step out in your business, you are going to meet various people who admire you for doing what they have been too afraid to do on their own. You will come across other businesses that offer the same or similar services as you; you will also meet others who have attained more success than you have. Knowing who you are, recognizing what your business model is, and having the stick-to-itiveness to remain planted is easier said than done.

Many times you are going to think that you must become like your competitor to win instead of fully fleshing out who you are. It is imperative that you don't lose your vision by trying to be something that you are not. Doing that will ensure your utter failure and success will forever be the dream unrealized. Your talents and gifts belong to you to be utilized in the way only you can and copying the actions of others puts you out of place, out of sync, and goes against 'your why' as an entrepreneur.

81

The more transparent I am in this book, the better it is for you. Yes, I had a purposeful dream before We Are B.O.S.S. LLC., and I allowed that dream to be corrupted by allowing it to happen; forgetting who I was and what my mission was. For me, this will always be the dream that almost happened but never did manifest fully.

In 1998, I started my first film production company, Devereaux Productions, Inc. (DevPro). I had written a screenplay entitled, "My Brother's Keeper" which focused itself around the music industry and an old relationship I lived through. As I began development with shooting my film, I met Lavon and Ravi after they auditioned for a part in the movie.

We three had become very close and were realizing that more exposure was needed to obtain the budget for production. It was at this time that Ravi introduced me to Kenya. Kenya had connections to the Hollywood scene and was very helpful in making it happen. We began to meet each week about the film's current production and we decided it best to stop it all together. We focused on putting together a performing arts showcase called, *"The Vibe"*. It was such a great weekly event at the time because Atlanta didn't have anything like it. We didn't pull it off by ourselves of course, we had the help of a hip-hop promotions company (The Committee), a video company, a local restaurant (Marco's Pita) that allowed us to host auditions every week, and Chris Tucker's Comedy Café that allowed us to host the event there every Tuesday night.

Through each of these connections the script was getting into the right hands and the exposure we wanted was really happening. It truly was mind blowing. The vision that I had for DevPro was within my sights. We were

82

invited to every industry party, function, outing…you name it, we were there! I was becoming known and there weren't social media outlets like we have now, it was good old-fashioned networking and working this business every single night…did I mention we all had full-time jobs too?

The descend began to happen after a one of a kind Hip-Hop mixed with Rock'n'Roll band auditioned for *"The Vibe"*. Ravi and I fell in love with this group. Of course, they made the show and we gave them a feature and treated the other acts as if they were opening acts for the band. After the show we all went to our favorite spot at that time, "Gladys Knight and Ron Winan's Chicken and Waffles" downtown. That was our official meeting location and they always gave us the Godfather booth, as I liked to call it. That night we learned so much about the band (I will not name them). Ravi, especially had taken quite a liking to them.

A few weeks had gone by and Ravi wanted to have a meeting with me. She told me of her desire to want to get into artist management and that the way she saw DevPro going, it wouldn't be the right fit but forming a full-fledged entertainment company would do it. I felt very conflicted because I had just started getting my second script, "The Perfect Couple" optioned and I had no desire for artist management. We needed to speak with the others and I felt that Ravi had put so much into DevPro that I should make this happen for her.

The meeting was set at our normal location and we began small talk. Ravi took the lead of the meeting with Lavon and Kenya totally in the dark of what was to come. As Ravi began to talk about it, it was then she brought up the conversations she had been having with the leader of the band we all liked so much. They needed management and gave us all the win-win scenarios that this would bring. Kenya looked at me and said, "Chanel, is this what you want? What about the films? Does this all just go away?" I remember Lavon just shaking his head because he was my best friend and knew my true heart's desire for DevPro. I was looking to find the words because I promised Ravi that I would back her up on this. I found my voice and even though I doubted it, I spewed the same rhetoric as Ravi. I told them that this would make us a greater force in the industry and open more doors.

We voted and decided to move forward with the artist management sector and that we needed to dissolve DevPro and reemerge as "Genesis Entertainment Group, Inc." Kenya was not happy at all during this process because she specifically came on board with her Hollywood connections to get a movie made, not to manage a non-categorized music band. Lavon got on board but felt that I was selling myself short into Ravi's dream. I was torn because all our time and effort went into making sure that the band was getting their studio time, developing a plan of action for them to get a deal, managing their rehearsals, ensuring that all bandmates were accounted for, and working on booking them shows. All the time that was dedicated to everything we were doing before ended abruptly. The films and scripts were pushed to the back burner, it was almost as if DevPro didn't exist anymore.

During all this work we were putting in, Kenya kept asking us to have them sign a contract. We were putting up all the money and time, the band was the only recipient of any benefits. They were getting their album completed, they were becoming more productive and cohesive as a group – the opposite of what was happening with us. We were constantly in discord with one another. I was growing unhappy because THIS is not what I started DevPro for and my vision was becoming Ravi's vision. At one-point Lavon came to me and told me that we needed to listen to Kenya and get the contract done.

Kenya hired an entertainment attorney who developed what we thought was a very fair contract to present to the band. We sent it over and didn't hear back from the band for over a week. That was weird because they would check-in daily with us. When we were finally contacted, they asked us for a meeting to go over the contract. It was a very chilly Thursday night in Marietta, GA at the rehearsal studio when it all happened. We each drove our own cars, pulled up and went in. Ravi, Lavon, Kenya, and I didn't say too much to each other, it's as if we knew something was wrong.

We walked in the room and the band members were waiting on us with another gentleman, but he didn't speak. We greeted each other but it was icy at best. The lead member started and told us that the gentleman was their attorney and that they felt the contract was too aggressive and they didn't want to enter into a concrete contract with us. They wanted to manage themselves BUT have us to still book their shows and we could get paid on the back end. Kenya got up, started getting her things and walked out the door. I was livid! Lavon, in his calm demeanor, basically told them that they wasted our time, used us to get positioned better and we wouldn't be booking any shows for them. He looked at me and Ravi, nodded his head for us to leave…I walked out without saying one word. When I walked out, I knew I had just thrown my vision to the trash.

Writing this story for each of you has me very emotional. It's 2017 now and Atlanta has become the second Hollywood. All of this took place in 1998 to 2000, and I was right there. I allowed the vision of another to infiltrate and takeover what I should have been doing. In my bio written back then, the last paragraph says this statement, *"Chanel Devereaux is making her mark in establishing a new Hollywood, here in Atlanta, GA!"*

That dream went unfulfilled because I allowed it to be corrupted by being someone that I was not. I will not blame anyone, as each of us who are entrepreneurs must be accountable for the decisions we make and what we allow to happen within the walls of our business. The influence to focus on what you don't do will always be there but it's in your hands as to whether or not you move in that direction. I am being very transparent in this section to let you know that you don't have to lose out and succumb to the pressures around you.

This very costly mistake is one that I have learned from. As a business owner, I have learned that every bad decision or failure can be turned around and viewed as an educational tool. Never allow your vision to be compromised or corrupted by becoming something that you are not or reinventing yourself based on anything other than divine revelation. If you are in the middle of a decision that goes against your business model, your talents and gifts, or your mission then don't make a move yet. Consider your gains and losses before you make that one pivotal decision. It's okay to say 'no', I've learned that NO is a complete sentence. *"Don't Allow Your Dream to Be Corrupted."*

STOP Do not proceed any further until you have done the below interactive exercise.

What is your business? What is your mission?

_____

_____

_____

What decisions or actions have you made that corrupted your mission?

_____

_____

_____

Write down the actions you will set in place to keep your business from being corrupted by outside influences.

_____

_____

_____

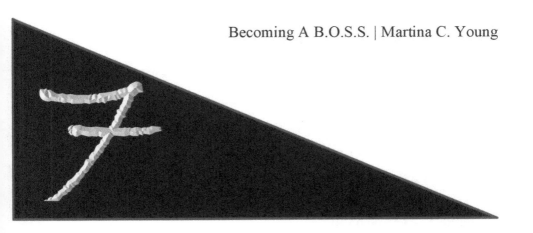

THE TEAM OF ONE RESULTS IN THE POWER OF NONE

The old saying goes, "It takes a village…" The same can be said when it comes to starting a business. Too many times have I seen a business with a great product or service go under because the business owner is a one man/woman show. They have the vision, put together the marketing, build the website, get the leads, make the follow-up calls, close the deals, do the work, yield the support calls, and on and on. These entrepreneurs are literally killing themselves to get things done, often not understanding why they aren't making any money and are losing clients.

We have all been there, you don't have the money to get everything done or to pay someone to do it, so you try your best to do it all yourself. While I understand and have been there, this mentality sets you up for failure. When you begin a business, it is important to get as creative as you possibly can when planning out what is needed to get the tasks done and build your clientele. If you start your business thinking all of the negative things about it then that's exactly what you are going to have! You cannot do everything yourself, there are ways to get more tasks completed without breaking your bank. Take a look at a few scenarios where entrepreneurs learned that the power of one will undoubtedly lead to the power of none.

Scenario 1 – The Scheduler

Marshall's dad had a residential cleaning service all this life and when his parents got older, they passed it on to him. He remembered how much his parents struggled with the business because they had to pay employees, buy equipment, and travel to the different locations. Marshall decided that he didn't need any staff because the business was in a financial situation. He planned it out. On Mondays he would conduct cold calls and follow-ups to interested clients. On Tuesday, he would use the morning to have meetings with interested clients. He would use Wednesday through Saturday as the designated days to perform the services.

Marshall's plan worked well the very first week. What he didn't foresee with his plan were the call backs that would come during the week while he was cleaning other residences. He knew that he needed to take the calls because these potential clients more than likely were calling his competitors as well. Marshall also realized that he couldn't be on his phone conducting business while he was cleaning a client's home. On his schedule he allowed two hours to clean each home and had the homes scheduled back to back and neglected to include the travel time between locations, lunches for himself, and gave no thought to clients who couldn't meet with him on Tuesdays.

His father suggested that he contact a staffing agency to clean at least half of the residences. This would allow him the opportunity to meet with potential clients and make call backs. Marshall didn't want to pay out any additional money, so he refused his dad's advice. He thought he needed to rework the plan and that he could make it work. After a month of going back and forth with his schedule, clients began to complain about the service. Many of them were not happy with the work being performed, they felt it was rushed. Marshall had to refuse new business because he just didn't have enough time in the day to do it. He wound up having to use his Mondays and Tuesdays to either make-up unsatisfied work or rescheduled clients due to his cancellations. It had gotten to be too much for Marshall.

The B.O.S.S. Evaluation

Marshall was setting himself up for failure when he thought having a plan to make a cleaning service work by himself would be successful. As children of full-time entrepreneurs, we tend to look at the failures of our parents and look to do the opposite of what they did. Marshall associated his father's struggles with an inflated staffing budget and had an inner desire to prove that he could turn the company around by himself.

When he went to his father for his advice, he refused it because that's what he felt was the ultimate downfall to the business. Marshall was unwilling to see beyond his own viewpoint. When you are in business for yourself, you must understand that you do not have all the answers. Your plan will not always work and must be trashed or modified. In a short amount of time you can lose everything you worked hard to gain by being resistant to change.

No one man can do it all. Marshall's situation proves that you can have a phenomenal plan that looks good on paper but real-life is unpredictable and in business we need to be prepared. Unfortunately, he wasn't prepared. By trying to save a few hundred dollars, it cost him his business and reputation. *"The Power of One Results in the Power of None."*

Scenario 2 – Lack of Backups

Raja owned and operated a construction company that focused on rehabbing properties that were destroyed by fire or natural disasters. Raja had a team he contracted to perform the services needed for the construction company as there was no way he could go at the projects alone. Outside of operating his construction company he was a financial advisor, sold health insurance, and started a handy man business. Raja was busy every single day. He had a wife and two children. One of his sons played baseball and the other played basketball. He was very active with his children and did his best to make every game even when the seasons overlapped.

Raja chose not to have a brick and mortar location, instead opting to have a home office where he did all the accounting and payroll. He used his basement as a storage for all the company's materials and deliveries. Raja built an additional room near the den for his home office to conduct business with the health insurance, financial services, and handy man business. Raja was doing okay with the construction company, but his other business ventures were not doing well. He could get prospects to meet with him easily, but he couldn't get them to convert over to full on customers. Raja had the necessary licenses to sell insurance and set up financial planning, but he was always lagging in responses.

He refused to hire an assistant to save money. Raja didn't even consider hiring a sales person because that was an even greater expense that he didn't want to share. It was common for him to meet with a client and they'd become confused because they came for one thing, then he would try to sell them on another thing. Raja needed direction as he became a jack of all trades and the master of none. That meant he had all the tools to earn money, but he lacked the resources to help the sales increase.

It was at one point after a hurricane that Raja missed taking a continuing education program for one of his licenses. He was literally all over the place. Raja couldn't get away from the work because something was always waiting for him at home. He had the means to get an office location, to hire an assistant, and to quiet his mind for refreshing. Raja didn't want to spend the money and then one day he got very sick. His body just shut down. Now, nothing was getting done. All his underdeveloped wells were running dry. While his wife stayed at home, she had no idea how Raja operated anything. The construction company finished all the projects that they were assigned but no bids on other work was done. Raja was so busy trying to build multiple streams of income without delegation or backup assistance that his illness brought everything to a halt. *"The Power of One Results in the Power of None."*

The B.O.S.S. Evaluation

Being an advocate of multiple streams of income, I won't give Raja a hard time about that. Not having a backup team or second in command trained in times of crisis will lead to a business failing. It is important that there always be someone else who can carry the torch when the owner isn't able to. Raja had a wife at home that he never took the time to even explain the basics to her so that if something happened to him she could run with it. Raja had a team with the construction company to do the work, but the organization's administration was done all by himself.

When crisis hit, his attempt to streamline his process without the help of others began to cost him more than he ever thought. I learned this the hard way. I was like Raja in many ways. I had to have that one element of control and then crisis hit at the close of 2015 that would leave me barely able to work my business for most of 2016. I wound up losing some clients because in certain aspects of my business, I was the power of one!

What I took from that experience is that it's okay to delegate and some delegation or shared duties is going to cost a few dollars. But if it saves your business, allows it to grow, then what did it really cost you? If anything, it frees you up to be the leader, innovator, and creator of your business that will ensure continued success.

Being the power of one isn't a thought that most of us do or say. It becomes what we do based on our thoughts of fear or complacency. We are fearful to increase our staffing/contracting costs, fearful that others won't do as a good of job as we can, fearful that our clients may be resistant to change, and other excuses you have. That's what they are...EXCUSES!

94

I know, I know, you are saying but they are legitimate excuses, and I am going to beg to differ with you on this. When you choose to be the power of one, you are operating in the place of FEAR. If you don't believe me, take a moment and write on the page all the reasons you are continuing to operate like an octopus. The next thing I want you to do is write why these are legitimate reasons and what you will find is FEAR! If you still don't see these as excuses, then visit: www.facebook.com/weareboss1 and let me know! *"The Power of One Results in the Power of None"*.

STOP Do not proceed any further until you have done the below interactive exercise.

I am not operating as the power of one because....

_____

_____

_____

_____

I recognize that my power of one is resulting in a power of none and these are changes I am going to make NOW:

_____

_____

_____

_____

WHEN PLAN "A"
DOESN'T WORK

Surely you are familiar with the flawed statement, "If you make a Plan B, it means that you are preparing for Plan A not to work." As you can tell I do not agree with that statement at all. Whether it is in your personal life or in business you are going to have an initial plan and it is not always going to go the way you anticipated to. The part that is frustrating is when people have their heart's desire on the way it should happen and when it doesn't, they give up or lose hope. The dissatisfaction of the ideology that you had in mind runs rampant. It then poses the question that we all have said, "Now what?" Have you been there? I can tell you that I have.

As an entrepreneur you are going to set goals that you feel can be attained with hard work and optimism. If someone were to ask you about your plan, you'd explain it as if it has already happened. You are certain that if you play your cards right, then it will line up perfectly. If you haven't experienced this yet, let me burst your bubble...IT AIN'T GONNA HAPPEN LIKE THAT! I wish that I could whisper sweet nothings in your ear but how would that help you? What I will do is help you prepare for the unexpected and not miss a beat in the process. Let's begin.

When you decided to start your business, you were told that you needed a plan. YOU DO NEED A PLAN! Did you think I would say anything different? Your first plan is going to be dependent on your business type, your personal goals, and anticipated strategy. This is a very personal decision that you would need to make. If you have business partners, then the goals that are set would be decided by you all collectively. If you are going at this alone and you work a job, then you may need to incorporate dual goal strategies that align itself with the regular job and the business creation. If you have left your job, working on the business and have children, then your first set of goals is going to be determined by your unique situation. Nevertheless, no matter what your situation, goals must be created. I would venture to say, 'attainable' and 'realistic' goals.

There is a difference in making a faith statement or affirmation verses setting an unrealistic goal. I am a big believer in speaking out what you see in your mind because that is the big picture or the result that you want to achieve. Just remember for every picture that is painted, it starts with one stroke of a paint brush. The Mona Lisa was not painted in two seconds. The design of your business is an artistry and what many people do not understand is that artists make many mistakes. They have perfected the tilt of the head to look at how they can mask the imperfection and then develop a strategy to fix it. That is how they review the details while working towards to the bigger picture. It's the same for your business in goal setting or planning. We establish the big picture and develop the steps (details) to

98

get there. That's why it is important that you don't set unrealistic goals because the details won't line up. Don't confuse your faith statement/affirmation with your planning.

We are going to use an avatar named Declan for the rest of this chapter. Declan works at a power plant in the evenings and has decided that he wants to open a dance studio for untrained dancers of all ages. He built a vision board that included his overall goal of having a fulltime location, ages spanning from kindergarten to young adults in their early 20s, all forms of dance categories and diversity. The first thing he determined is that he needed to find time in the day to put together which programs he was skilled to teach, a location to use, and which age group to begin with. Everything had to be built around his work schedule because that would not be changing any time soon. He had worked that schedule for the past five years.

After months of planning, he had everything in place to begin his first two classes. It was perfect. He would get home in enough time to get at least six hours of sleep, conduct the classes and have enough time to sleep before his shift began again that night. He planned to have a big event to kick it off, he almost sold all the open slots for the starting classes prior to the opening. Nothing could stop him...except his job.

Declan was called into a meeting the night before the big event and was told that his position was being eliminated and to keep his job he would have to move to dayshift. Declan was mortified. He was in no position to quit his job and everything that he put in place was based on a schedule he had for five years. Plan A was his only option. Let's stop for a moment.

Have you ever had a clear and concise plan and then out of the nowhere came the greatest obstacle that seemed to ruin everything? This is what happens when Plan A doesn't work; it doesn't mean its forever ruined, it means we have to divert ourselves to a different path to get back on track. It's an emotional rollercoaster because now you have so many things to consider and not sure which way to go with it. This is why we don't only create one path to get something done. What if this were you? Would it be over in an instance? Would you throw your hands down because it seems like things just never go the way that you want them to go?

Certain things are not within our control and we must be prepared for it. I carry an umbrella in my car every day, even if there isn't a cloud in the sky. I keep it in the car at the chance that I would be caught out and it did in fact rain. I may not be expecting rain every day, but I am prepared in case it does. Do you have an umbrella in the car for your business plans? Plan B or Plan C doesn't mean you have failed or that it's not going to work out for you, it means you have a backup plan in case there is a glitch in "Plan A".

This monkey wrench thrown at Declan doesn't mean he has failed, it is what he does next that determines if it failed. Plans are just that…plans. They do not have the ability to succeed nor fail, we do. Our decisions, our preparedness or lack thereof is what determines success or failure. Have an honest conversation with yourself as if this were you. What would you do in this regard? Would you rise to the occasion and figure out what to do or would you just cancel everything? This is an exercise. To benefit from it fully you must complete this portion before you start reading again. No one else is going to see it, it's you learning to be honest with yourself. This is to help you grow so DON'T CHEAT!

STOP Do not proceed any further until you have done the below interactive exercise

Based on the scenario with our avatar, Declan…what would be going through your mind and how would you handle it?

_____

_____

_____

_____

These are the thought processes you have already gone through when your Plan A didn't work. There isn't a right or wrong answer at this point unless you threw in the towel, but even that is subjective because that determines how committed you were to make this dream a reality. Now, I would like you to take a moment to write down what your Plan B would have been and why. This is another exercise that you need to be honest with yourself on…NO CHEATING.

_____

_____

_____

_____

_____

Let's continue with Declan…

Declan walked out of the meeting feeling defeated. Everything he poured himself into making happen felt like it was being taken away from him in an instant. However, Declan knew in his heart that this had to work. He wouldn't let it beat him. Going to a day shift position would make it more difficult but if he stopped then all his planning and time would have been in vain. He went home after his shift and didn't make a change to anything. The next day, he went through the event without a hitch. He still had no idea how he would pull this off, but he figured something was going to work out.

He was talking to a woman who inquired about a job as a dance instructor. At that moment, Declan had an idea. It was his Plan B. If her references checked out, then maybe he could have her conduct the classes in the day time and he could now open the evening classes that were once not even on the table. This was his Plan B.

Declan's ultimate goal was to have the dance company profitable enough that he could work the business full-time. The Plan B option meant he would have to pay out a salary to this person, but it would also open a revenue stream for the evenings and he still had the classes he was going to do on the weekends. This also gave him the idea that if she didn't work out, he could still post up an open position for a dance instructor to teach the classes while he was at work. Declan's vision was limitless again. He still wasn't thrilled fully that what he envisioned needed to be altered, however, he had a concrete plan on how he could get through the setback and turn it into a set-up to accomplish the things he truly wanted.

Setbacks are going to happen but it's how what we do with them that determines the outcome. In Declan's situation he thought of a Plan B, he didn't have one established at the time. It was because his attitude was one that said, "I am going to make this work in my favor!" At first, he was devastated as most of us would be, but he didn't let himself stay there. He got out of his emotional head, and stayed in the game.

In doing so an opportunity availed itself to him. Nothing would have been wrong if he made a contingency plan either (Plan B). It would have given another way to get to Plan A should something change it up. Again, I do not agree with the statement that says if we create a Plan B, we are expecting Plan A not to work. If you don't give up or lose focus on what Plan A is then it doesn't matter how you get there! Just get there!

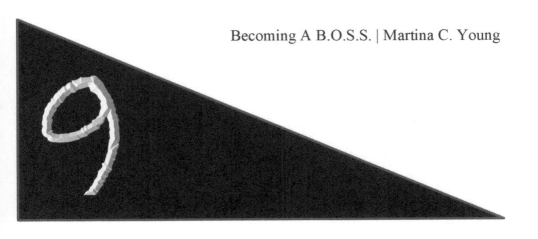

SAY GOODBYE TO THE 'YES' PEOPLE

You are the smartest person I know, everything you do is right, that was a brilliant idea, I know you ran into the wall but still great job…AUGH! We all love compliments and flattery! There are individuals that can make the vilest of people feel angelic about themselves. When is enough, enough? As an entrepreneur it's okay to have those individuals around but not to the point of them being a hindrance. These are called the 'Yes People'.

'Yes People' are building blockers. They do not challenge you, they want to build you up so much that even your wrongs are good. You cannot grow a business with a group of these individuals around you constantly. Your family and friends are usually your most honest audience. They will tell you when your food is bad, when you need to fix your hair, change your clothes, and in some cases, bathe! I am not speaking on 'haters' but those who have your best interest at heart. The same is to be said for your

105

business. When you begin your entrepreneur's journey, you may have it all thought out and you think it's great but someone close to you may see a flaw or mixed message you are sending. Our first reaction is to greet them with a prideful indignation. We may say to ourselves, "who made them the judge?" Let's examine that for a second.

Family and friends are also your customers. Again, I am not speaking on those who are coming from an envious or jealous place, I am just speaking about truth in general. These people will tell you what the public may not share with you or will share with you in a very viral negative review. For instance, I had set up something on my website a few months ago. I was pleased with it overall and then I got a call from one of my colleagues and pushy-pushers, Jonathan Wofford. He called to tell me that although everything looked good, I had too many steps for potential clients to register. He told me that my message wasn't coming across the way it needed to and that if people couldn't get in and out, then I was going to lose sales. I was frustrated because I had worked tirelessly to make it easy and now here is Jonathan telling me I failed because it was still too confusing.

It's because I trust him and know that he would never steer me in the wrong direction, I made the changes and it did in fact help others to maneuver on the site more effectively. Now, by the contrary, when I showed another person they felt it was perfect. They didn't want to hurt my feelings and became a 'yes person'. 'Yes People' can cost you business without even meaning to, they are confidence boosters and there is a time and place for them.

As an entrepreneur you cannot afford mistakes because someone didn't want to hurt your feelings. 'Yes People' are innocent looking, toxic individuals who don't mean any harm, but they do cause damage. When you are investing your money and time into building your product and you need an honest opinion, having someone that is only going to stroke your ego will be very costly for your business. A few years ago, someone I knew wanted to start a catering company because people had told them how good their food was and that they could make a lot of money doing it. I had tasted a few dishes and the food was good the first time on the plate, but it was weighed down with so much grease that you could make yourself sick if you ate too much. In addition to that her vegetables were always over cooked. She kept saying how she wanted to serve her food to a higher end clientele and I told her that she would need to rethink her recipes. She got so upset with me and said she didn't want to talk to me about it again. I know I have a way with wording things, but I had to be honest.

Instead she pursued her catering company and couldn't book anything that she went after. The others around her told her that it was good and that she didn't need to change anything because that's what people like to eat. Her menu didn't sell. I am not saying that I had all the right answers, what I am saying is that her prideful indignation prevented her from exploring other recipes to make her product more appealing to others. When her business flopped, the same people who were telling her not to change a thing were now saying that maybe she should have changed up some things.

There was a time in my life where I had nothing but 'yes people' around me. No matter what I did or said, I was always great and so smart. Then I met my match in Ronald T. Young, the hubs. He also thought I was smart, as a matter of fact he says all the time that I am the smartest woman he knows. There was a problem though, he is smart too and can match wits with me. When we started dating, I didn't realize that I had become used to people giving me very little push back and embracing my ideas or concepts. He would cause me to think beyond the obvious and it would annoy me to my core. The bible says that 'iron sharpens iron' and he had a way of doing that. It was a question or statement he said to me that made me realize that I needed to get these 'yes people' out of my life. He said, "Am I the only one telling you this? Are people afraid to challenge you?" I remember getting in my car going back to my apartment thinking that same thing. There wasn't anything for him to gain at the time, we weren't married at the time and he wasn't involved in any of my businesses. I had to get very honest with myself and realize that I was allowing these people to hold me back by telling me what I wanted to hear and bullying them with any other response...Tina's way or the highway. Thank God for being delivered from the 'yes people'!

Don't get me wrong, having people who build you up in your corner is needed. They are good for those bad days when you want to sit and have a pity party. In your business endeavors though, 'yes people', can stifle you if you allow them to. It all comes down to what you allow in your life. When you only surround yourself with people who tell you what you want to hear by tickling your ears then you never realize what you need to improve upon. Too many times, myself included, have blamed others for what I allowed to happen. Growth is painful, it is uncomfortable, it is challenging, it requires strength and understanding. Kick the 'yes people' out of your life when you are attempting to grow...YOU will be better for it!

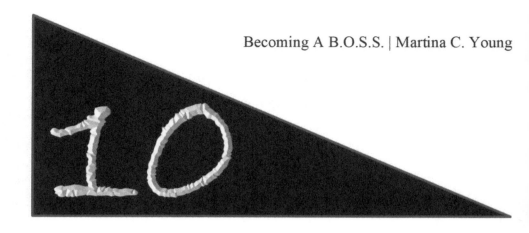

DON'T WORK FOR FREE – FREE HAS A PRICE

When you decided to become an entrepreneur, I can bet you didn't get into business to work for free. You didn't think you could leave your job, pay your bills, or send your children to college by working for free. No one gets into business to work for free, not even if you start a non-profit organization. You are looking for financial freedom. Setting your financial goals did not include doing a bulk of free work while others enjoy or make money based on your work. This is where you have the responsibility to ensure that your clients, friends and family understand this principle. Free comes with a price and you are the one paying it.

How you begin your business is how your friends, families, and clients will see you. Most entrepreneurs start out trying to bait those close to them into using their products or services, so they give insanely low deals that equate to pennies on the dollar or no money exchanged at all. This is NOT how you want to start your business. I know this to be a fact.

Developing your price model is one of the first things you need to do and stick with it! When I first started out building websites, I made this mistake. I didn't have a price model, I had a 'fear model'. I was fearful that no one would pay me what I was worth because I was just starting out. I also had the fear that the target market I was going after didn't have the money to afford normal pricing. So, I offered the most insane deal and now it makes sense why I had all of this business and couldn't realize a profit. I began building websites for $299 that included: free hosting, a free domain, unlimited graphics for the slide show, up to 25 editable images, unlimited pages, and unlimited revisions. Then I only charged $50-$65 for maintenance fees per month, on demand! The hours that I put in for each website left me making $.60 an hour and a few projects I didn't even make an hourly wage that was calculatable. It was crazy! It was as if I was working for free! If I had truly done a few things first, I would have saved myself two years of pure headaches.

STOP Do not proceed any further until you have done the below interactive exercise.

A few things to consider in effort to avoid underpricing your products:

1. Write out all your services, what it takes to perform each one, the anticipated time to complete them, potential hiccups that may arise, and if it takes more than one person to do it (contracting someone else).

_____

_____

_____

2. Research at least three of your competitors and get a gage on what they are charging for the same or similar service.

_____

_____

_____

3. Calculate what your desired hourly wage for each service will be. Be sure that you do not use a range, but determine a concrete number.

_____

_____

_____

4. Calculate any overhead that you must maintain to produce the service or product. This will include internet fees, office rent, utilities, insurance, licenses, business phone, etc.

_____

_____

_____

This is your starting point. You can look at what it takes to perform the service or make the product, know what your bare minimum per hour that you need to make, understand how much you pay in expenses to determine how many gigs you need to complete each month to cover the overhead, and be competitive in your market with those offering the same services. When you have done this, you will see that FREE comes with a price – YOU pay that price.

Never allow yourself to undercut your value when you know that you have a reputable product. There are always people who have the means to pay your price. You should never work for free! If you have gotten your business off the ground working for peanuts as I did, then stop it right now! Regroup. Discounts should not be given out the way Oprah Winfrey gave out cars! Your clients should earn their discounts by either the business they spend with you or by the referrals they send your way. When you go to certain grocery stores, you must own a rewards card to earn discounts on groceries and fuel. I have a Gold Membership at a popular coffee house. They don't just give me free coffee or pastries, it depends on how much I spend, and then I earn the rewards.

You are not required to give free services to family members and friends. This is a HUGE mistake that many entrepreneurs make. The philosophy is if you look out for them, they will look out for you. Unfortunately, that is not always the case. It takes the same amount of time to perform the service for family and friends as it is with public clients. I'm not saying that you never give them discounts, I do but I do it when I am able to do so. If I have a full client load, then I may not be able to give them

113

a discount because the time is being used for fully paid clients. Discounts should be used as rewards and not expectations.

Client expectations and pay policies are important. Each business is setup differently so the rules of how clients should pay you may be different. In my industry some services are required to be paid in full, a few services require a 50% deposit which is what covers my full labor costs and the remaining is due within 14-days regardless of completion of the project, and some are on short-term monthly recurring charges. For your business, all of your payments may be due upfront or at the end of the deal.

Be sure that you set a standard and stay with it. The first time you detour from it, you can be rest assured that you will have a reminder of it in the future. It is very important that you know your value and your worth without apologizing for it. Every single time that I have ventured outside of my rules to help someone, I have gotten burned in the end. Every single time. Remember, that you don't have to work for free and that free comes with a price that you will pay for in the end. *"Don't Work for Free – Free Has a Price"*

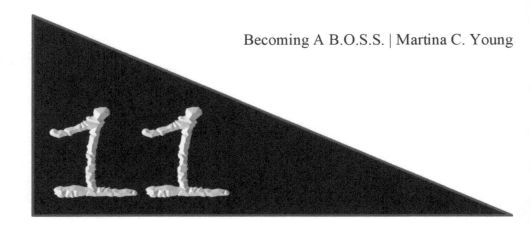

ARE YOU MISSING YOUR TARGET?

Many entrepreneurs float aimlessly never really knowing the market that they serve or who their customers are. This is called defining your target market. When you shoot a bow and arrow, you don't just shoot it in the air. You point it at a target, *usually a red dot encased inside of a circle,* it's established that you want the arrow to land dead in the center. It's the same with your business.

The product or service that you developed is set for a certain target. Your business is the arrow and the red dots are the consumers you anticipate conducting business with. Every product or service isn't going to be a good fit for every person. If you never define your target market, then you will never have effective marketing. It is imperative to know who you serve and how to reach them. When you don't know who you serve it is a sign that you really don't know your own product or service.

116

Let's look at a few true stories of entrepreneurs who could not identify their audience and the results. Maybe you will find an 'ah-ha' moment for yourself.

Scenario 1 – Lack of Understanding the Trend

In almost every conversation that is being had in business and in the news today, people can't stop talking about the Millennials. Millennials are changing the way we market, setting the standard for the way we use technology, they are living more carefree then generations before and they are setting trends that make professional arenas more casual and friendly. Walter retired from corporate America and moved to a very progressive neighborhood to open a dry cleaner's shop. He looked at the residents and realized where he was located was primarily made up of people that were thirty years his junior. Walter did everything he could to market his business to the millennial population nearby. He invested in a commercial that had 'hip' music, held community events that he thought would appeal to that group, and he even tried to hire staff that met that age range. He could not understand why he would only get a fraction of business and when they did come in, they would drop off one or two items. When he had dreams of the cleaners he envisioned his customers dropping off their families' suits, shirts, dresses, slacks and all. That wasn't happening. He had a few baby boomers who would use him for their Sunday suits or their annual dry-cleaning needs but the market he went after was unresponsive.

At his wits end he sat his younger staff down to ask them what they thought the problem really was because if he didn't figure it out soon, his whole life savings would be gone, and he'd have to close. One of his part-time employees said this to him, "Most people that I know rent their clothes and send them back. They don't need them cleaned. This is a monthly service that is used so people my age who don't have a lot of money can have new clothes and never repeat an outfit." Walter was floored! He had never heard of such a thing and that his young staff spoke it as if it was common knowledge. It all made sense to him now. Walter was going after a market that he knew nothing about while he gave no marketing attempts to the target market that still valued and had constant need of a neighborhood dry cleaners service.

The B.O.S.S. Evaluation

Walter could have avoided a lot of wasted time and money if he had taken the time to learn his customer. Hearing popular terms or phrases are easy to influence your decision when determining which target market to pursue. You have to figure out if your product or service truly matches that market or not. In this case, he had been hearing about Millennials running the world and thought by moving his business in an area where they dwelled would force them to use his services. What he didn't expect was for them not to have a fully established need to use a dry cleaner. This is a very common mistake the you want to avoid.

When you look at your product or service, really think about OR research who will be spending their money regularly with you. Forget about what's trending or what's hot! This may mean putting together a focus group. A focus group is pulling together a group of people that meet the ideal avatar (customer) and getting their feedback. This will save you a lot of time and even more money. Walter spent money on a commercial and based it on what he 'thought' would attract the target market but instead it was money thrown in the trash can. After all that he spent, he found out in one quick conversation that he was out of touch with the target market he was pursuing.

Even though there may be other reasons, that one statement showed Walter that he had made a huge mistake. Does this mean that he should just close his business? Absolutely not, this is the opportunity for him to hire a marketing team to help him define his target market and launch a marketing campaign to that group. You can always re-examine your strategy and make the necessary changes to correct your mistakes.

Think about your business for a moment. Place at the forefront of your mind the target market that you feel you serve OR the target market you would like to serve. Imagine those people in a room where you have put together your own focus group. What would you ask them? What information would you attempt to gather? Use the below to write out your answers:

_____

_____

_____

_____

_____

If you have never used a focus group, shame on you! Now you will have the opportunity to. Within the next 30 days, you should build upon and organize a focus group for your business. Where are you lagging in business? What do you want to change? What does your customer want? When you have completed your focus group and have your results, visit: www.facebook.com/weareboss1 and let us know how it went.

Scenario 2 – I'll Do It My Way!

Cheryl and Alyssa wanted to open a bakery in a very popular plaza in the Atlanta area. The surroundings were very progressive with people riding their bikes to the store, sidewalks filled with families taking neighborhood strolls to the local eateries, small cafes and a bookstore. There weren't any fast food restaurants instead they had local grocery stores, pop-up farmer's markets, and many vegan-based bistros. This was a community that cared about healthy living. Cheryl and Alyssa came to that area every day and had a self-realization that what was missing was a bakery. The pop-ups carried some baked goods but not the type of items that they would offer. They went into the grocery store and noticed it didn't carry an abundance of sweets that were very tasty.

Cheryl spoke to the bakery manager and he told her that most of the requests he gets are allergy friendly baked goods, low sugar or sugar free options, and vegan based cakes and desserts. Alyssa had a few recipes that were diabetic friendly and felt that she could offer recipes as alternative options. Cheryl felt that they didn't need to change a thing unless it was requested.

After about five months, they moved into the location. They had a huge, festive community based grand opening. It was so much fun. They had samples of cakes, pies, cookies, and other specialty items. Cheryl nor Alyssa were prepared for what would happen next. They were bombarded with questions about the ingredients in their baked goods. The customers wanted to know if they used refined sugar, pure cane sugar, sugar substitute and if so was it generic or stevia? They asked about the use of eggs, were they free range or steroid free; they needed to know if the flour was bleached or whole grain. Were their desserts gluten free? It was at that point Alyssa knew they had made a very big mistake.

The B.O.S.S. Evaluation

There is an old saying used often, "Follow the money." Unfortunately, as an entrepreneur that is not always the case. Cheryl and Alyssa thought that the plaza they selected was the right fit because the money was steady and that they established a need. They never took a deep look at their product and compared it to the behavior of the people that lived there.

Cheryl knew that she needed to check the bakery climate by visiting the stores and pop-ups to see what her competition was doing. Alyssa recognized that the residents were very health conscious which explained why a lot of the desserts they made were not being sold in abundance. They missed the mark because they ignored the facts. When you are getting ready to find a location for your business you have a lot of factors to consider and it's not about the money being passed in the area.

Ask yourself a few questions:

1. Is my business a fit for this environment?
2. Is my product or service needed in this area?

3. Do I need to modify my business model in order to fit in?

These three questions will help you get started. These are preliminary questions every person should ask themselves when starting a business and choosing a location. Take a look at your business and ask yourself the same questions. Use the below to write out your answers:

_____

_____

_____

_____

_____

Think about your answers for a moment. *How did you determine if your business was a good fit? Did you think about the number of competitors in the area? Are they earning income or is there high turnover in your business category? Are you comfortable with changing some procedures or product variations to fit the market? How costly would the changes be to your business? Will the changes you have to make compromise your business model or will it enhance it?*

Three simple questions came with more questions behind them. If Cheryl and Alyssa had done this before opening the business, they would have more than likely decided against the location. Their business wasn't for the health-conscious family, it was for people who enjoy their guilty indulgences. They opened their bakery and served the wrong demographic.

It will be utterly pointless to begin your business and/or find a location if you have no idea who your customer is. The foundation of getting your business going is knowing who you serve!

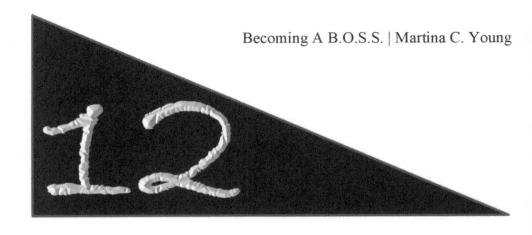

SOCIAL MEDIA WILL SAVE US, RIGHT?

There are so many misconceptions about social media. While it is a very effective tool with getting your message out, it is not the only tool to use when it comes to marketing. If Social Media were a person, we would dress it up in a black cape and call it a hero. When I am speaking with people about their marketing plans, it is either in the first or second sentence that they begin to rattle off about their social media presence and followers.

My question then becomes, "How many of your followers are actual clients?" What is the purpose in going viral to a million people if less than ½% of them conducts ongoing business with you? Hey!! Before you get all huffy with me, I will come back to your *many followers* and how to use them as leverage…no matter what you say, if they are followers and not conversions then it isn't as successful as you may think!

By definition of social media marketing as defined by Techopedia states, "Social media marketing (SMM) refers to techniques that

124

target social networks and applications to spread brand awareness or promote particular products. Social media marketing campaigns usually center around: Establishing a social media presence on major platforms." Notice one thing, it did not say that this was to be used to guarantee conversions and sales for your business. Social media is a tool to help garner exposure, introduce you or your business to an audience you wouldn't be able to ever meet on your own. The key word is that its 'social'. This means not everyone that is coming on any of the social media platforms is always in the business mind.

People come on social media platforms to connect with old friends, family, be nosy, check out the latest gossip news, etc. A lot of users get on to get away from business or work. There is a method to making social media marketing campaigns work for you, but you must understand that this isn't the only way to market your business. It may be one of the most cost-effective methods but if you still lack the necessary marketing foundation, then you still will not yield conversions.

Social media marketing is directly connected to your activity on those networks. How many friends or followers do you have? How often do you post? What is the activity on your business page? These things matter. If you have a social media account with 30 followers, you only post once or twice a year, and you don't engage on anyone else's page, how successful do you think your marketing campaign will be for you?

I encounter people who tell me that they have a page, but they don't 'get on it like that', but are expecting 20,000 people to just up and purchase their product through a sponsored ad. NO ONE KNOWS YOU!!! Unless your product is the most unique, brand new, never been tried but desired in the world, people aren't just going to spend their money with you! Social media marketing takes work. All of us wish it were that easy to just spend a couple hundred dollars for a social media campaign and become millionaires overnight.

Social media marketing campaigns can be productive. I use them myself and have had concrete conversions not just people who engaged by liking or commenting on my page, but purchasing my service! They spent money with me. The basics of my marketing foundation was already in place and that's what I am going to share with you now.

Let's demonstrate how to make social media marketing work for you. We are going to start with a quick quiz. Are you ready? Even if you are not, give it your best and DO NOT CHEAT!!! Don't look ahead. Do not use Google or Siri to do this activity. Phones, tablets, iPads...DOWN! (I see you.)

List your definition of a marketing mix.

_____

_____

_____

_____

Okay, now write down what you think the 4 P's stand for:

P_____ P_____ P_____ P_____

If you are not sure, it's okay. I want you to give it a shot anyway. When you began your business, you weren't sure about it, but you did it anyway.

Think about four factors that MUST be considered in any type of marketing you have thought to do or have done.

Defining the foundation of your marketing is going to always come back to your marketing mix. Your marketing mix is a combination of the four Ps that must be fleshed out in order to begin your marketing strategy. They are comprised of product, place, promotion, and pricing. Without the establishing these four elements, you will undoubtedly fail to market your product effectively. If you have never identified this for your business, you have no business running a social media marketing campaign.

The product is the most important to define. This is your actual product or service that you have based your business on. Clearly defining your product is key. This includes what it does, how it operates, what it looks like, determining its true value, its personality, making it a full-fledged entity.

Place is speaking of your distribution methods or strategies. Where can people get the product, how will you get it to them, what's its availability, is it online, do you have to be in person to get it, if service based what's the accessibility method, etc.

Promotion is your plan on how you are going to market the product. Does this mean you are going to do direct sales, online sales, advertise on television or on social media, advertise in a magazine, mail out flyers, stand up in a mall and scream!!! Promotion are your plans to promote!

Pricing is something we touched on in an earlier chapter. What is this going to cost your customer? You must be sure that your pricing includes the money you have spent out on product development, placement costs, promotion fees and your profit margin. Pricing is one of the factors that seals the deal as to whether potential clients would like to use your services or not.

Okay, now that you have a brief understanding of a marketing mix, let's go back to social media marketing campaigns. If you have ever run an ad on social media before, do you remember having to answering a ton of questions? They wanted to know your marketing mix. They needed to determine the product you were offering, the target market that you want it sent to, what your plans were to get it to the customer, and how much you were willing to spend. The marketing mix is always there.

As an entrepreneur, you must be able to fully answer these questions. If you cannot, you shouldn't be doing any sort of marketing. If I had one million dollars for every time a person told me that they spent tons of money in social media marketing and nothing happened, I would be a billionaire!!!! Often it is because they lack the foundation needed to capture the audience they are targeting.

Back to those who have tons of followers. If you have a large number of followers who are not conversions but simple engagements, then you must revisit if your followers are actually your target market. If you determine that they are not your target market then you should reposition your ads that get them to buy your product or service for another person, give away as a gift, etc. You can still leverage off a great number of followers. But you have to go back to your place and promotion strategies, so you can hit that affiliated target. Think about the times you have bought something online for another person. That ad targeted you to do exactly what you did, it didn't target you to buy for yourself but to buy for another person. It's all in your messaging…we'll get to that in the next book!

STOP Do not proceed any further until you have done the below interactive exercise.

Write down every social media platform you are on. Next, write down which you use for business and which you use for personal.

_____

_____

_____

Overall, what is your social media presence saying about yourself?

_____

_____

_____

Based on your posts, frequencies, and activities with others, would others view you as someone playing or conducting business? Why?

_____

_____

_____

Open the conversation up about Social Media Marketing on our Facebook page! Visit: www.facebook.com/weareboss1.

<u>EPILOGUE</u>

Thank you to each one of you that invested in yourself to purchase this book. The development of this book was a very grueling process and one that I will not forget. The life lessons that I learned in business have helped me to become the business coach that I am today, and I had to share it with other entrepreneurs in the only way that I know how...raw and truthful.

It is my heart's desire that you were able to find nuggets of information that will help you in your business and in your life as an entrepreneur. My delivery is very straight forward and never to offend but to challenge you to be your best in business. Always think about how you would want others to see yourself and then behave that way. Remember that you may mess up a time or two but as long as you have breath in your body, you can always get it right.

The life of an entrepreneur can be very rewarding and if you take the time to do it the right way, you will reap the rewards. Remember that it takes a lot to run a business and if it doesn't happen overnight, that's okay. Plan A doesn't always work the way we think it should, maximize your Plan B and get back to Plan A in the right timing!!!

We Are B.O.S.S. LLC., was my 17th business! My Plan A didn't work out, but I kept pounding the pavement until it did. Setbacks don't stop you from moving forward, you do. Always remember that. In January 2019, look out for the next book..."The Entrepreneur's Guide to Getting Your Business 10-Figure Fit!"

Use these next few pages to write updates and progress to the areas you needed to address in other chapters.

_____

_____

_____

_____

_____

_____

_____

_____

_____

_____

_____

_____

_____

_____

_____

_____

_____

_____

_____

_____

_____

_____

_____
_____
_____
_____
_____
_____
_____
_____
_____
_____
_____
_____
_____
_____
_____
_____
_____
_____
_____
_____
_____
_____

About the Author

Martina C. Young is the entrepreneur's trainer for business and marketing development. Many of her clients have referred to her as a walking business dictionary. Her story is much like that of many entrepreneurs. She knows the hustle, the faith walk, the setbacks, and the focus needed to build a business from the ground up. In 2008, she had enough of working as a Corporate Trainer and Executive Administrator and left Corporate America.

Martina C. Young is a dream activist and pursuer of what others deem to be impossible. She is an expert in the field of business development, marketing planning, strategic marketing, integrated marketing communications, competitive analyses, and financial projections. She is an accomplished business coach, public speaker, and Co-Founder of We Are B.O.S.S. (Business Owners Striving for Success) LLC.

Martina C. Young

Twitter: /weareboss1

Instagram: /martinacyoung

Facebook: /weareboss1

Website: www.martinayoung.com

Email Address: gettrained@martinayoung.com

Phone Number: (404) 857-BOSS (2677)

Martina C. Young

c/o We Are B.O.S.S. LLC

2295 Parklake Drive Suite 550

Atlanta, GA 30345

(404) 857-2677

BUSINESS & LIFE COACHES

SPORTS PROGRAMS

NETWORK MARKETERS

REAL ESTATE AGENTS

BRAND NEW BUSINESSES

An online interactive Business and Marketing Development Boot Camp designed to GROW, EXPAND, and CREATE REVENUE for your business! In 12 short weeks, you will receive exclusive weekly training videos, course assignments, targeted discussion boards and detailed feedback. You will also receive LIVE strategy sessions with Martina Young, preferred pricing for ALL We Are B.O.S.S. sponsored events, as well as additional VIP perks!

New Sessions Begin:
Every First Monday of the Month

Get enrolled TODAY to reserve your seat at the table!!!
Only 20 seats available per business category.

Enroll at: www.martinayoung.com

MARTINA YOUNG